UNFROZEN

A FATHER'S REFLECTIONS
on a BRAIN TUMOR JOURNEY

UNFROZEN

A FATHER'S REFLECTIONS
on a BRAIN TUMOR JOURNEY

TOM MATSON

Mill City Press
Minneapolis, MN

Mill City Press, Inc.
322 First Avenue N, 5th floor
Minneapolis, MN 55401
612.455.2293
www.millcitypublishing.com

ISBN-13: 978-1-62652-876-5
LCCN: 2014908350

Cover Design by James Arneson
Typeset by Biz Cook

Printed in the United States of America

CONTENTS

AUTHOR'S NOTE

In November of 2011, I was frozen in the game of life. Many of us have been frozen in our own games of life. In those moments, the game continues around us, and we sit frozen and searching for someone to help us thaw. This is my journey of becoming unfrozen.

I've written this book to my children, Morgan and Tyler. I want the two of you to fully understand my journey and the ways my view of life continues to change. By no means have I figured it all out, but I have learned some things that I hope will impact you today and in the future.

One

My Hockey Haircut

Dearest Morgan and Tyler,

This is the story of my brain tumor and a difficult season of life, but first, we need to talk about hockey and sports.

I'm going to start by wowing you with boldness. The following words will shock and awe you. You may even need to take a break to catch your breath. Here it is: your dad has never been the quickest of athletes. I don't know why I'm telling you that since I've passed on that same speed (or lack thereof) to you. I guess I should apologize, but what can I say? Matsons just aren't fast. We are fun, good communicators, and can maybe even play a mean triangle in the band, but speed is something God gave to others. The challenge is that we are Minnesotan, where everyone is born with ice skates on their feet. In fact, both of you were given skates shortly after you were born.

Like many kids in Minnesota, I was a hockey wannabe. I imagined flying along the pond with my mullet—which we called a hockey haircut—flying in the wind and scoring the game-winning goal like Mike Eruzione. (If I have to explain who he is, I'm going to make you watch *Miracle* for the 100th time). Of course, the problem with my *Miracle on Ice* dream was that no matter how many speed-skating courses I attended, I never got any faster. Your grandma would tell me that I had other good qualities. Yet no matter how many times she said that, my hockey dreams never went away.

I suppose my love of hockey started because I was born into the family of a hockey coach. When I was roughly six years old, your grandpa helped coach a Junior hockey team to a national championship. During the cold winter months, he would flood our backyard and set me free. I had a chair to hold onto as I skated, along with the giant oak tree in the center of my personal rink. I would skate out there for hours on end.

All and all, I would guess the rink was roughly ten feet wide, but in my world, I was playing in Madison Square Garden. The lights my dad had hung from the tree certainly added to the effect of spotlights on me. But those darn lights were loud when they hit the ice after I skated across the extension cord. I guess that just added to the excitement.

I grew up in a city known for its hockey history. I remember going to the Minnesota State Hockey Tournament with my friends in junior high. The impact that moment had on my life is why I spent eight years on a waiting list to get season tickets to that same tournament that we enjoy so much today.

That first year, my friends and I got to watch Neal Broten, Phil Housley, and other famous hockey names compete in front of 120,000 screaming fans over three full days of hockey. I still remember watching the 1979 State Tournament live on TV while on spring break in Florida, with Howard Cosell as color commentator. That trip was the first time I had ever been on an airplane and the first time I had ever seen the ocean, and I sat inside watching a high school hockey tournament.

The tournament's "Cinderella story" that year was, and always will be, the Roseau High School Rams (a true small town). They played against the larger schools, of which the most famous and most hated was my (and your) hometown: Edina. The Edina Hornets have won more state championships than any other high school in Minnesota. Plus you can't get much better drama than small town vs. big city. It was always interesting to tell people I was from Edina. They would ooh and ahh about how rich Edina was. I playfully loved to tell people that we just pulled in our camper and rented a P.O. box in Edina, but they never bought it.

The reality is, I didn't grow up with much money. There were some lean years for us as a family, yet I was reminded how much love wins over financial resources. I grew up loving canned tomato soup and cheese slices on white bread. My mom always made sure I had everything I needed. As you have experienced with her, she always provided, and it was always through a lens of love. She bought my jeans at Sears; they were called Toughskins, which was basically a stiffer jean material with patches built into the knees so you could rip through the denim and still wear them. The problem with that design was that as you washed them over and over, the jeans would fade, and the patch in the knee would become even more obvious. That wasn't a big deal in elementary school, but when I got to junior high and was one of just a few still wearing them, it was safe to say it created some insecurity.

To add to that insecurity, I had stopped growing. I had always been tall and somewhat ok in sports growing up. I had great coordination and was blessed with an awkward, rare combo: I had short legs and a long torso, which meant I was hard to tackle in football and could catch anything thrown my direction. Of course, that whole lack of speed thing ruined my NFL dreams, but I still had a good athletic body. However, that just wasn't true in junior high when I went from tall and lanky to short and chubby. Suddenly, I wasn't good at sports, and I was insecure about my body that had more to love. Clearly this was a season of life that your dad was at his very best.

I still remember 7th grade when the trend shifted. Toughskins were completely out, and even though I hadn't moved up to Levi's yet, they were too. I was *two* jean steps behind, which is clearly a junior high nightmare. So there I was, feeling chubby, slow, and lagging in the jeans world.

But I was smart and creative. Although some may have called that "awkward" in junior high, I thought my creativity made me unique. I mean, not everyone in 7th grade had mastered the Commodore 64 and Nerf basketball—*and* still loved Legos.

One day I showed up to school and noticed a horizontal white line across the denim above the zipper of everyone's jeans, and I knew my Toughskins were in trouble. These cool jeans were a new Italian line starting at $79, which was far more than we could afford. So your creative dad went home and found a typewriter whiteout sheet.

Sadly, I don't think you have any understanding of a typewriter. (I still sweat profusely if I think about keyboarding class.) If you made a mistake while typing, you would insert this thin plastic sheet that had a type of white paint on the back, hit backspace, and type the incorrect letter again to erase your mistake. So I took off my pants and carefully used that whiteout sheet to draw a white line across the zipper of my Toughskins. I was "in" and "hip," and I put them back on and walked out to show my parents, who tilted their heads, looked at each other, and drove me to Dayton's five minutes later to get my very first pair of fancy jeans. I know they couldn't afford it, but sometimes that's what parents do. To show how much I loved them, I wore them every single day. How could you go back to Toughskins when you had felt that soft Italian denim on your legs?

Every day I would show up to junior high with my fancy jeans and do the very best I could in school. Now, the older the two of you get, the more certain teachers will begin to stick out in your memory. As you both know, I believe teachers are the true pillars of education. They create a world in which students feel celebrated, challenged, and better than when they arrived for the day. My favorite and most life-changing teacher was Miss Horseman.

Mrs. Horseman was the first teacher that made me feel smart. She taught me to write—in fact, she told me daily that I was a gifted writer. One of the best words she ever taught me was *oxymoron*, and to this day, I love seeking words or phrases that are opposites. (*Jumbo shrimp* was always my favorite.) In my life, I understood the tension of things that simply felt like they didn't fit together. In my particular case, a family that wasn't loaded with money yet loved hockey felt like one such tension.

The good thing was that my dad knew everyone in Edina. Both my mom and dad grew up in the community and were as networked as anyone could be. To this day, my dad still has his old routines. He drives daily to Wally's Gas Station to talk to Rick, Wally's son. It's truly a small-town gas station in the midst of the city. At Wally's my dad picks up his Diet Mountain Dew and his paper.

Often after Wally's, he loves to stop by city hall, and on this particular day, he had brought me with him. While at city hall, the Parks and Rec director brought us back to a giant storage locker full of old, used hockey equipment. We dug through the piles until we found equipment that mostly fit me and sort of matched. I know my parents were stretched because of paying for my hockey, but they never let on, and I never complained about my equipment that looked nothing like the modern gear of my teammates.

Tyler, I tried to introduce you to hockey at a young age. In fact, I got you started playing hockey at the exact same age I was when I began. In Edina, that's called the Mites league. I'm proud to say that was the one trophy I won playing hockey. Not everyone can brag that they won the Edina Mites Hockey Championship. In fact, I still have the trophy proudly displayed on my workbench (which may or may not be a sad thing to admit).

While I wanted you to have the same hockey experience I had, this is one of the many times your dad messed up: I started you too late.

Nowadays, parents start dreaming of state hockey championships for kids who are far younger. By the time I got you involved in hockey, most of the kids had already been playing for two whole years in a new program called Termites. Needless to say, your skills just weren't at the same level as others'.

However, you didn't let that stop you from being you. I still remember sitting outside in the cold Minnesota night watching your very first game. I had come from the car, where I gathered all of my winter gear including my hot cocoa. The action on the ice was on the east side of the rink. I watched all the players skating together like a swarm of bees chasing that little black puck, each player with steam rising up from their helmet. I searched to find you within the pack. Out of the corner of my eye, I saw you. Instead of walking across the ice (which is what your skating amounted to back then), you had decided it was a perfect time to chat with a friend.

You rested one arm on the goal at the west end of the rink and had a nice long chat with your new friend the goalie. Line changes were simply time away from that chat, and no matter how many times the coach encouraged you to go to the puck, the joy was in the conversation for you. Oh, how that moment revealed how you think and what you value. There were lessons for me to learn that day. No matter what is taking place around you, you still love quality time with another person. Even if that quality time is almost interrupted by a hockey game.

Morgan, your hockey career lasted a whole year longer than Tyler's. Your challenge was always being more interested in where I was watching from in the stands than what was going happening on the ice. You know me: as a lifetime coach, I always had a hard time sitting with the other parents. I found it exhausting to hear the endless complaining about the coaches, refs, and other players while watching a game of fourteen-year-olds doing the best they can. Instead, I would stand off to the side by myself so I could watch in silence and simply celebrate that you were out on the ice as you attempted to play a new sport.

Maybe that's why you loved to search for me. Maybe it felt like a Where's Waldo? game to see if you could find where I was stand-ing—but I suspect there was more to it. You've taught me to not let my identity be thrown off by the competition and how it was so fun to share with someone you love. Sadly, I've seen far too many athletes, parents, and coaches lose this valuable gift you've given me. Their highs and lows are impacted by what takes place in the midst of competition. Though your hockey career didn't last long, you taught me to share what matters with those I love.

Because of all I've learned about life from both of you, I know it's meant to be shared with friends, and I have found life thrilling as I search for the gift of authentic friendships. I'm not naturally social, and I find most social situations exhausting. If I had a choice, I would avoid such moments like the plague. When I'm forced to be in social situations, I want to get there early or find a helpful job of some kind. In my limited mind, if I have a role to play, then I have a reason to appear busy and antisocial. Even once the party starts, I love to stand by the food so I have some-thing to talk about. But sometimes, in the midst of a social ocean of people, we are given the gift of friends we deeply connect with. My friend Steve is one such a friend. Not only was he a coworker but he was smart, authentic, and kind. Plus—maybe even most of all—he was a hockey fan.

A year after meeting Steve, he asked me to be a part of his men's USA Adult Hockey league. It was full of a great group of guys who loved hockey, and yet, many hadn't been playing for that long. I was so excited when he called to ask me that I went downstairs to try on my high school hockey equipment. I guess my body has shifted a bit as I've aged because suddenly I felt like Chris Farley in *Tommy Boy* singing, "Fat guy in a little coat." Plus, my equipment was completely outdated. My glove had a giant rip in the palm, and if I wanted to restart the hockey career I never had to begin with, I needed to at least look the part.

So I ran to the local hockey store and loaded up with all new equipment for the new chapter of my hockey career. Our first practice, ironically, was at the home of the Richfield Spartans, the team that ended my Hornets season over twenty years earlier. It was a late-night practice, and I was leaving for California to speak at a conference the next day. But I didn't want to miss a chance to play with my new group of hockey friends, so it didn't matter how late it was.

When we hit the ice, it took me a bit to get a handle on skating with all that equipment and playing organized hockey again. I had a hard time skating with my head up and found myself running into people over and over. My first two shifts consistent of me trying to not make too big of a mistake in front of my new hockey friends. On my third shift, I was carrying the puck down the left side of the rink, and I attempted to make a pass to a charging teammate on the right. I remember thinking that I was finally starting to look like a hockey player again; I was skating as hard as I could.

As I passed the puck, an opponent lunged for it. Instead of hitting the puck, his stick's blade became lodged in my skate. The next thing I knew, I was flying through the air, landing perfectly on the right side of my head and shoulder.

Dazed, I lay there for a few seconds and made my first aid instructor proud by doing a mental body check to make sure nothing was broken. Understanding that I hadn't broken a bone, I slowly skated over to the bench. My next shift out, I skated around for what felt like ten minutes before returning to the bench. I was nervous my teammates would think I was hogging the ice, and I wanted to make sure everyone got to play equally. But the looks from my teammates suggested they weren't happy with how much time I was spending on the ice. Weeks later, I found out that what I thought had been ten-minute shifts actually been closer to ten-*second* shifts, but my brain wasn't exactly registering what was taking place in that moment. Something wasn't right.

The next day I left for University of California—Irvine where I spoke to an amazing group of 250 student leaders about their leadership strengths, engagement, and well-being. I found myself sweating more then I was used to and constantly losing my place in my talks like never before. In addition, I couldn't find my car in the lot after the conference; I lost my bag at the airport and couldn't remember where I parked my car at the Minneapolis airport once I had landed at home. I had to call airport security and drive around with them until I finally found my car. Simple memories were suddenly out of my reach, and I had a headache and dizziness that wouldn't go away. While driving home from the airport, I called my family physician and forced them to get me into an appointment that day.

My doctor is one of those that makes you feel better about yourself and feels like a true partner, no matter what you are dealing with. He is also a team doctor for the Minnesota Wild Hockey Team, which clearly elevated his status in my mind. We talked for a while as I explained my headaches, memory issues, sweating, confusion, and more. He diagnosed my symptoms as a major concussion and ordered an MRI for me that day. He also called a neurologist to meet with me a few days later to talk about my symptoms and MRI results.

That was the first MRI I had ever had. Though I had had two concussions growing up, that was long before MRI machines were invented. As they slid my 6'4" broad-shouldered frame into the MRI, it felt like I had been shoved into a claustrophobia-inducing casket. My heart began to race as panic took over my body. It felt so out of control and scary, and with my head surrounded by pillows and a cage over it to hold it in place, it was more than I could handle. I hit the button for the assistant to come hold my hand. I boldly said, "If you don't hold my hand and calm me down, I'm going to throw up in your machine, and I ate a big lunch." Her warm hand calmed me enough that I was able to shut my eyes. She encouraged me to imagine I was on a beach somewhere, and the heat and noises were simply a part of the amazing vacation I was on. I shut my eyes and kept them shut the entire forty-five minutes. I was frustrated that I had to go through an MRI at all when the results would show that I had a concussion and nothing more.

Two days later as I was driving to my neurologist's office, my phone rang. I recognized the number as my family physician's and assumed it was my family doctor calling to talk about my MRI results. Something you should know about me is that whenever I have the smallest of symptoms, I go to the doctor. I figure if something is wrong or could be wrong, I would rather know sooner than later. So I would often assume the worst only to be told I had a cold.

Ironically, this time I was expecting my doctor to say my results looked good and that my neurologist would help me with some at home exercises I could do to bring healing to my brain. I'd had my bell rung many times playing sports growing up, and I figured this was no different. However, I instantly knew this was a call like no others.

The doctor's normally playful voice was calmer and had a greater sense of urgency to it. He talked about how MRIs work as he slowly walked me through the medical jargon as he shared what I knew was bigger news. Sometimes I appreciate medical history and facts, but I certainly didn't on that crisp October day. I had tuned out for a bit when, suddenly, I heard his words loud and clear.

The MRI had revealed a brain tumor, an acoustic neuroma or vestibular schwannoma, as he medically referred to it. I couldn't fully take in what else he was telling me, but I remember hearing "cranial surgery or radiation," and the call ended as I parked my car in the neurology clinic's parking lot. The next moments were a bit of a blur as I walked in slowly, checked in, sat down, and replayed the conversation in my mind.

I was suddenly overwhelmed by emotions like never before. My throat began to tighten and my face felt warm. My emotions were rising up like a volcano ready to erupt, and I could do nothing to stop it. It started with tears and deep, painful breaths as I relived his words. My sobbing became deeper, and I didn't know where to turn or how to hide. The rest of the people in the waiting room simply stared at me while I kept saying these words out loud, over and over: brain tumor, brain tumor, I HAVE A BRAIN TUMOR. A new phase of my life began that day: a journey that started with a hockey game and ended in a calm-to-chaos moment of life.

Two

The Right Words

I've always prided myself on my ability to communicate. Heck, I've focused my entire professional life on using words. But not just any words: the right words.

I've always found words fascinating. Growing up, I loved playing Scrabble and Boggle with my mom. To this day, I sometimes write such a perfectly flowing, articulate e-mail, I have a hard time sending it. I wonder how I can release those perfect words into the hands of others.

Sometimes my fixation on words gets in my way. I can listen to an hour-long talk and obsess about a few words that rubbed me the wrong way; that fixation holds me back from truly enjoying the talk. In addition—and I'm a bit embarrassed to say this—as a speaker, I'm critical of other speakers. I try not to be, but it sneaks out, often at the very worst times. Weddings and funerals are two times that are supposed to be for reflection and celebration of life, yet there I sit, overanalyzing the words I hear from the speaker.

My fixation on words also impacts how I parent and communicate with the two of you. I think that's why I enjoy teasing you when you use the word "like" so often. Just last week when I was talking with you both after school, instead of truly listening, I was nodding my head and secretly counting the number of times you said the word "like." For all I know, you shared something profound, and sadly, I missed it due to my own amusement.

So you see, words matter to me. The right words. The perfect words. After my name was called in the neurology waiting room, I was ready to hear the words about what my future may look like. My neurologist looked first at my MRI, then my red eyes, and tried to slow down his words to appear empathetic. But I wasn't looking for empathy from a stranger. I was looking for authenticity. For me, authenticity has always been the ultimate way to gauge a leader's impact and influence. I wasn't in the mood for "fempathy" (fake empathy). I wanted and needed him to simply speak the truth.

Maybe that's why, when the two of you leave for school every day, I say, "Be you." The people I love to be around the most are authentic and comfortable in their own skin. On that day, I didn't need to visit a counselor rather I wanted a factual doctor. I guess that's how I am during times of high stress. I want facts, learning and understanding more than anything. Someone who knows more than I do calms me and calms those scary emotional waves.

My neurologist presented two options to me on that day. First, I could do some sort of radiation (at least that's what I understood at the time) or second: cranial surgery (which sounded scary). There are times when I simply don't know what to ask, and this day was one of them. The only other time I can boldly remember not understanding what question to ask was the day you were born, Morgan. I had never done this baby thing before! Yet somehow I knew I would be ok and that I wouldn't mess up too badly. I had been used to not always knowing the right question to ask, and I've always felt comfortable with that.

But that day felt different, and as I sat in front of my doctor, my lack of questions scared me. My shortage of questions wasn't coming from a place of confidence like the day Morgan was born; they were coming from a place of fear. I knew I couldn't just keep staring at the doctor, so finally, I quietly said, "Tell me about cranial surgery."

In my mind, that felt like an easier answer to hear about than radiation. Plus, since I hadn't fully heard what he said about radiation, I wanted to appear like I was paying attention, and those words "cranial surgery" still were hanging in the air. Ten seconds into his answer, I figured out why I wasn't ready to ask questions: I wasn't ready to hear the answers.

Cranial surgery is as scary as it sounds. However, I learned it was the best way to understand the nature of the tumor. The tumor could be fully removed and tested to best understand its makeup. Neurology is an amazing profession, but it's a guessing profession, too. Since they can't see, touch, and feel the brain and the inside of our noggin, they do the very best they can to guess—and they're pretty darn good at it. Removing the tumor would allow them to know if it was cancerous or not.

"Is it cancer?" was the question a majority of people asked first. In fact, I've been asked that more times than I can count, yet to this day, it still feels like such an odd question to receive. Some asked because they wanted to know how to respond to me while others asked due to their own curiosity. I hoped it wasn't cancer. The doctors tended to guess the same, but we had no way of truly knowing unless it was removed. Removal provided answers and great risk, side by side.

I've never been good at risk. I wish I was, I really do, but unknowns scare me. It reminded me of one summer, when ten of my closest friends and I packed up our woodie station wagons—a car as wild and sexy as a minivan—and headed up the Quetico, which is straight north in Canada.

The Quetico is a chain of hundreds of clean, beautiful lakes, most accessible only by canoe. We had reserved our campsite months ahead of time (sight unseen, obviously), and as we canoed around the corner, we were met with the most beautiful view ten college men could hope to see: a fifty-foot-high cliff directly off of our campsite. There was a long silence as we stared at God's majestic playground. Finally, my friend Scott said what we were all thinking: "We need to jump off of that."

Now, you may think your dad was nuts to consider jumping off that cliff. That's a fair thought, and you should know I considered not jumping. I looked over the edge and saw some rocks, plus the cliff's face was angled out, so I had to jump really far—and not only am I slow, I'm also not a strong jumper. I didn't want to jump, but I did . . . once.

I didn't feel pressured by my friends; it was something I needed to do for me. I needed to rise up to take on my fears head on, and in the midst of a close group of friends, it felt like the safest time to do so. I remember my hair flying in the wind. The jump felt like I was falling in such slow motion that I had time to look around at my friends below. But what seemed liked twenty minutes in the air was only a few seconds.

It wasn't the jump that stood out the most; it was the landing. Right when I launched myself into the air and off that cliff, I thought of the Mountain Dew commercial that had come out that summer. It was a group of friends jumping off a rope swing into the water with their arms outstretched (like the letter T) as they did so. I figured I would emulate their style for my pictures of the jump, but I didn't think to compare the height of their jump to mine. Just like they had done, I landed with my arms outstretched, and those arms slapped the water louder than the sound of thunder. Not only that, my new neon orange swimsuit that I had thought was so trendy was up to my chest! Plus, there was water where there shouldn't be water! Someday you may understand the word "enema," but on that day I understood it very clearly and uncomfortably.

But, I did it: I jumped when others from our group weren't willing to. Your risk-averse dad went for it. Sometimes we just need to jump in life. Those can be the greatest moments of growth. Now, I do want you to think and be smart, but learn from the fear in life that has at times held me back. Please jump. Take smart jumps and safe risks.

While the cranial surgery would indeed provide answers, was it worth the jump? The more questions I asked my neurologist that day, I certainly wondered if it was. Key phrases from the conversation stood out and tainted my view. Maybe it's not that his words tainted me, they just scared me. I can honestly admit that today, but I struggled to at that stage. I felt vulnerable, suddenly a bit fatter, a slower, and more flawed. I probably hadn't gained weight and was as quick as ever (which I realize is slow), but this darn tumor made me feel broken.

Irrationally, I wanted to run away right in the middle of that neurology appointment and I was feeling waves of fear crashing everywhere and anywhere, and I needed a safe harbor. Sometimes, however, life doesn't provide us with a safety net. We are called to keep going, even though we are hurting, wondering if we can really make it.

While I was looking for my safe harbor, all I could hear and feel were the storms erupting around me. But I know that if I'm patient enough, storms will eventually be silenced. Maybe that's why I've always loved mountain storms the most. They are dark, loud, and scary, yet they move through quickly. My neurologist's words that day felt like a mountain storm.

The thought of having my head opened up sounded like a horror movie. First, I was told that following the cranial surgery, I would definitely have short-term facial drop. Oftentimes the brain is so amazing that it figures out how to how to "talk" to those muscles again, allowing the face to work right over time. But that wasn't a guarantee. In fact, the chances of cranial surgery damaging the facial nerve long-term were high due to the way my tumor was situated.

Second, the chances of losing my hearing were high. For someone who loves the sound of a mountain stream, birds, and music that scared me. Finally, the statement that threw me off the most was this: "Most people regain their balance within a year." When you aren't a fast or incredibly athletic person, balance is often all you've got going for you. Plus, as a tennis coach, balance is fairly important. Cranial surgery would have taken me out of work and life as I knew it for nine to twelve months before I could get back to a place where I could work and function normally again. Can you believe how much time? That would include roughly two weeks in the hospital and time to let myself heal. I know it's been the right decision for thousands of others who are living amazing, functional lives, but sometimes what is right for others may not be right for you.

Ironically for someone who loves words, as I drove home from the doctor's office that day, finding the right words proved to be impossible. I called a few of my loved ones, but the minute I heard their voices I began to cry and so the conversations were short. I waited until I got home to tell your mom. I watched the fear in her eyes as I told her as she processed my future and yet her own as well.

After I had talked to your mom, I drove to my parents to tell my mom and dad while the two of you were still at school. While I had felt strong and stoic with your mom, telling my parents felt emotionally overwhelming and shortly after the words came out of my mouth, I began to cry. No Parent wants to see their child suffer and I could see the fear in each of their eyes as I shared my news. Like so many others in similar positions, I ached to take action and fix their fears while also removing myself from my state of helplessness. I guess no one wants to be stuck on an island of fear. I could feel myself spiraling, and I didn't know how to stop my slide. To be honest, you two, I didn't know how to tell you, and I know that was a part of my slide into darkness.

I think the two of you knew something was wrong the second you walked in the door after school. We had you sit down and share my news while watching both of you process in your own unique way. Tyler, you went up into your head to process what I was saying while for you Morgan, the tears began to swell in your eyes. No daddy wants to look flawed or broken and I tried to share as much as I knew at the stage.

That night our lives continued on as normal as it could feel, but I started a new habit of laying with you as I tucked you into bed, and asking if you had any questions or new feelings. What we began that night, we continued throughout this journey and I promised you that we would make choices together. I promised openness and transparency and that we would make choices that would honor our family values.

This process reminded me to make choices that are honoring of you and how you think and feel. Make your decisions based on research and time spent processing with those you trust. We only have so many chances to jump off those cliffs, so pick those moments wisely and trust your heart. It's often in the moments when we are most aware of our needs that the storms cease and we feel the true peace and gifts of life.

Three

Frozen in Life

I've always loved playing games and I grew up in an time that weekends were spent playing neighborhood flashlight tag and recess was a time to enjoy the classic playground games. I loved a game that allowed everyone to continue playing even after they had been tagged. I guessed that's why I struggled with freeze tag so much when I was younger. The whole concept of being frozen and unable to play the game until someone touched you to unfreeze you was really hard for me. It probably had something to do with a game of freeze tag I played at a family-type camp when I was a kid. We were playing freeze tag at night out on the basketball court that was lit by one giant light. In one moment, the game shifted to the far side of the light, and one of the younger boys got stuck on the far side of the court, on the other side of the light. He had been tagged.

He stood there, frozen in his running stance, and yelled for someone to tag him so he could play again, but with the game so far away on the other side of the light, no one was close enough to unfreeze him. I remember the panic in his voice as he realized the game was continuing without him. Finally, in his ache to play the game again, he began to cry from the pain of missing out on the fun. Then I saw him appear out of the corner of my eye: it was the boy's father. He walked slowly over and touched his son's shoulder, letting him play the game once again.

Your mom and I will sometimes do the same to the two of you in life. There continue to be moments where we feel frozen and unable to play the game of life. It will be in those moments that I will take this big hand of mine and touch your shoulder and remind you that you can play life again. I'm also wise enough to know there will be times, as I get older, that you will do the same right back to me. Life is funny like that. We enter into this world helpless and often leave the same. The simple, loving touch of those who love us is what brings peace to our lives along the way.

In this stage of life, I needed the two of you to remind me that I was still loved and not frozen. I found myself comparing my life to the lives of the people around me. I wondered why I was at this spot and I felt depressed. Now, I realize I shouldn't admit it to all of you, but on this particular day after hearing about cranial surgery, I was thinking about those in my life and past who had it worse than me. And in my depressed state, the first person to come to mind was my classmate Kari.

Kari is someone from my past who has often been at the forefront of my mind. I wish I could say it's because she was the top jock, the smartest, or most popular, but in this case that sadly wasn't true. I didn't really get to know Kari until high school, but we were introduced on the playground years earlier. Kari had a different body type than so many of us at that age, and she was born with a top lip that was slightly deformed looking. She was quiet and often walked alone on the playground, counting down the minutes until the bell would ring, forcing us back into our prison and her freedom. When Kari was around, suddenly I wasn't the slowest kid or the lowest on the social totem pole.

I remember one particular day at recess with the sun upon our necks, the sweat beading down our backs as we ran around on that sand-covered playground. The sand was kicked everywhere and anywhere as we moved our feet in any direction possible to avoid getting tagged. That day, the words being used forced us to move a bit faster and stealthier.

"GIRL GERMS!" Karen yelled as she touched my shoulder. Karen always wore Minnetonka Moccasins. The kind that have that soft leather wrapped around your feet with one simple leather tie around the ankle. On this warm spring day, her moccasins didn't seem fair to me. Those soft leather shoes made her a playground ninja, and she tagged me before I even knew she was there. Her aggressive tag caused me to tumble forward onto those rocks (thank goodness my Toughskins had those built-in patches). I jumped to my feet to find someone to tag, and there was Lynn. She didn't see me coming from around the wood playground platform and cargo net that separated us.

Lynn was my dream girl. Actually, I think she was everyone's dream girl at that age. There she was, and I was ready to tag her. My fake

Vans (a skateboarding shoe) with the checkerboard top proved to be the perfect shoe to move upon that sand. Each baby step moved me closer and closer until finally I reached out and screamed, "BOY GERMS!" as I tagged her arm. A life lesson was learned that day: don't scare the person you have a crush on. Her look of fear after I screamed in her ear was a look no person would want to see again.

But the thrill of the game and my lack of self-awareness in the moment forced me to quickly keep running and keep playing. The game had been about boy germs and girl germs. But suddenly, my friend Jim changed the rules, adding a new wrinkle to the game. He yelled out, "Kari germs."

Jim's words hung in the air as we all processed what he had said and done. Now, I wish this was a proud moment for me. I wish I could tell you that I stuck up for Kari and stopped the cruelty. I wish I could tell you that I was that boy, but sadly, I wasn't. I let the game continue, and I watched out of the corner of my eye as Kari processed what she was seeing and hearing. A tear slowly dripped down her cheek as she turned away so we couldn't see. She walked up the hill to visit her mom who was a teacher at our school. The game continued that day for all but one of us. While the words weren't used directly, I think Kari was frozen on that day. Like that little boy screaming out to play the game of life again, and yet the game of life continued without her, and none of us had the courage to unfreeze her.

The game of life continued for all of us as we grew and developed. We got a bit older, a bit wiser, and a bit more self-aware. I think Kari was in my middle school after those playground moments, but I can't say for sure. Sometimes we live so deeply in our own world and our own needs that we fail to see what's going on around us. It reminds me of the great teacher John Keating played by Robin Williams in the movie *Dead Poets Society*. In the movie, he says, "I stand upon my desk to remind myself that we must constantly look at things in a different way." Yet in my insecurity during school, I failed to shift my perspective, and I missed moments and people that could—and should—have mattered.

The greatest thing about the game of life is that along the way we have teachers and mentors like Mr. Keating who seek to love, impact, and inspire. Those teachers that ask us the right questions, the hard questions, and genuinely care to hear the answer. One of the mentors in my life believed in me so much that he handpicked me to attend a leadership retreat. Over the weekend, we learned about our unique strengths, followership, and service leadership. To further make the point about service leadership, there was a group of fellow high school students working behind the scenes to make sure every detail of the weekend was perfect. We didn't see them, but we knew they were there because each of us had one assigned to us. They would write in our leadership diaries when we weren't in our classroom and tell us wonderful things about ourselves. To this day, those are some of the most loving, tender words I have read about myself. They remain in my "pick-me-up smile file" to read on those hard days when I wonder if I'm doing anything right.

"Tom, you are a leader that leads through a lens of servanthood and grace," one of the notes reads. Another talks about why I'm loved, and yet another about how I impact others. This servant leader poured into me and filled my bucket. On the last day of the retreat, the servant leaders introduced themselves to all of us, one at a time.

"Tom Matson, please stand up," and I waited to be introduced to this amazing, gifted encourager. There I saw her: Kari. This amazing person who had poured into me all weekend was the one I had let wander alone, frozen through life so many years before. In the midst of my tears, I hugged Kari and said thank you over and over while also apologizing.

Was this tumor going to define me and freeze me like Kari had been frozen so many years ago? No. I wasn't and I'm not frozen today, but I've had to remind myself of that mindset daily. All of us will have our challenges in life, and all of us will, at some point, wish for a "normal" life. In the movie *Tombstone*, Wyatt Earp went to go see his friend Doc Holiday as he lay in bed, struggling to take his final breaths of life. In a whisper, Doc drove a conversation that's never left my thoughts. It started with a simple, authentic question that any one of us would consider on our deathbed.

Doc Holliday: What do you want [in life], Wyatt?

Wyatt Earp: Just to live a normal life.

Doc Holliday: There is no normal life, Wyatt. There's just life. You live it.

Wyatt Earp: I don't know how.

Doc Holliday: Sure you do. Say goodbye to me . . . and don't look back. Live every second. Live right on through to the end. Live, Wyatt, live for me.

The hand I've been dealt isn't perfect, but it's still life. Kari kept on playing the game of life, and so will I. One day at a time, one step at a time. I realize some of those days will be painful and scary, and I'll need those safe harbors, but the game of life will go on. This tumor didn't define me, and I wasn't going to be frozen in life because of it. I wanted to keep playing, but I did need to make some decisions.

Four

Flexing My Presidential Muscle

The Internet is a dream come true for those of us who love to learn new things. I can't even begin to count the number of times I've been in a meeting where someone says something so deeply interesting and new that I mentally checked out for the rest of the talk. It's not that I'm permanently zoned out, but their words created an unspoken need to research and learn more based on what they said.

Like both of you, I love to learn. I love facts, and I love to know something new each day. Tyler, you have always been driven by that same need. Notice that I call it a need and not a want. Every time that need is fulfilled, I can feel the joy rise up in my stomach. It's been interesting to watch you and seeing how your need to learn impacts you socially and scholastically. Every single time you shared that you were having struggles at school, it was due to other kids distracting you from your learning. You would communicate their rudeness and lack of respect for you, others, and the teachers. But at the end of it all, those darn kids were keeping you from learning! How dare they?

Sometimes my learning needs remind me of watching the *Merv Griffin Show* with my mom growing up. On one particular show, Merv had a group of body builders on as guests. Of course, they came out oiled up, tan, and wearing speedos that allowed every muscle to be seen. Their muscles glistened in the light, and every pose and step highlighted a different muscle group. I saw muscles in spots I didn't know muscles existed. It's funny that even when I played college tennis and was forced to lift weights daily, I've never had muscles that glistened in the sun. Heck, I live in Minnesota, so I've also never had a tan that would boldly show off my non-existent muscle tone anyway. But these body builders sure did, and I sat next to my mom watching their perfectly toned bodies until finally, Merv walked over to them, smiled, and asked one simple question: "So what do you do with them?" It's a fair question, but they chose to respond with actions rather than words. They simply posed again. He smiled kindly and asked them again, "But what do you do with them?" Of course, they paused and posed yet again. The exchange went on one more time until Merv finally smiled again and gave up.

Often my need for learning feels a bit like those body builders. I get distracted by a love of learning new things, and, like those body builders, there are days I wonder what I'm going to do with all that knowledge. Yet somehow, knowledge feels like power to me. When I can grab ahold of research, thoughts, and learning, it creates hope. During this time of my life when I felt so out of control, hope is exactly what I needed.

So I poured myself into researching acoustic neuromas and reading about what others had done in my situation. I wondered if this was wise; my friend Mark, who had previously gone through his own medical issues, guarded against it. Maybe he was right. Early in my research, I was drawn to anything and everything written about brain tumors, and that lead me to personal blogs, reflections, and more. Honestly, what I saw and heard scared me.

You see, I was still at a place of comparing cranial surgery to different types of radiation treatments, so I read about seizures, saw pictures of cranial scars and facial drop, and the heard all about the consequences, until one day I simply needed to stop. After days of reading all of those blogs, my emotions were out of control. I remember wondering why all of these strangers wanted to share such personal things. What drives that in someone? Is it based in the need to help others, or the need for attention? Was it the healing power of therapeutic writing, or people trying to get their feelings and thoughts out of them for the world to share in their burdens?

What a different age we live in that people feel comfortable living their lives so publicly. Pictures, words, and thoughts are put out there for the entire world to experience. I wonder what the outcome of such a world will be. That's one of the things that has been interesting for me to watch with the two of you. When I ask you to talk to a friend, teacher, etc. you will choose to text or e-mail over a phone call. Am I letting you down as your father by allowing that to take place, or has that become how the world is? The challenge for me is knowing that someday you will need to interview for a job and you won't be able to text your responses. You'll actually have to use spoken word and show non-verbal responses as you communicate. So please, know the emotions a smile generates when you talk. Please know the power of a firm handshake and great eye contact. Finally, never forget to be authentic to who you are. Be you.

I also want you to consider the daily resume you are building within social media. One reason I have avoided so many of those social media sites is that I worry I would say something I wouldn't be able to take back. I have this side to me that is quick to think, and my words come equally fast. It's made me a wonderful and dangerous debater. Ironically, that combination is one of my biggest strengths, yet sadly, it can also get in my way. It reminds me of a story I once read about someone who was far quicker and a far more impressive debater then your dad.

President Lincoln was authentic and fast thinking, yet from what I have read, he had a quick temper. He knew the dangers of that combination. While President Lincoln didn't have to deal with Twitter, he did have to deal with his weakness head on, and he used his strengths to do so. He strategically created a habit of allowing himself to write letters while he was angry and his words were flowing. I can imagine the aggressiveness with which he would attack that letter and the pressure his pen would put on the paper. I have no way of knowing this, but I suspect that old, wooden desk of his was indented in places from his aggressive writing.

We all know what it's like to feel such strong emotions, but it's in those moments that we are reminded how out of control they can make us feel. But our wise former president did, and boy, would it force his pen to paper. He would write words that were full of emotion and possibly anger and boldness, words he may have regretted—that's why he wouldn't send the letter. Did you hear what I said? He never sent those letters. Not a once. You see, President Lincoln knew something I think many of us forget today. His words were so deeply powerful that he had to find a way to control his emotions so they didn't harm others and himself. So he took those emotional letters and threw them away. Ironically, you feel a certain level of freedom after getting those emotions and words out.

So Morgan and Tyler, please think before you speak *and* write. Your words matter. They are a powerful sword and can cause equal damage as a true weapon. That's what's scary about this new age of technology: we don't have the chance to write and throw away. Your words, pictures, actions, and possible regrets are out there for the entire world to see. That includes not only your immediate family, but also future employers and even your own children someday.

I've attempted to put that same healthy mechanism into practice in my own life, but I wish my smartphone were as smart as it claims to be. If it were, it would send me a warning when I was about to send an e-mail or text response far too fast and without thinking. While I've learned to set my phone down and walk away before responding, there have been many messages that I wrote with tremendous anger and almost sent but didn't. Maybe I should have sent some of them, as I realize that anger is a true emotion given to us by God, but often walking away from the message was the right thing to do.

One of my most challenging moments was on the day of your seventh-grade flag football championship, Morgan. I wasn't there;

instead I was traveling for work and hating every second of it. Honestly, your team hadn't exactly been amazing going into the playoffs, so I can admit that I didn't think your team would make it to the championship. But there are moments when teams come together perfectly, and your team had done exactly that.

I had skipped going out with a group for dinner and instead sat eating in my hotel room while receiving texts about how your game was going. I can admit to you now that I knew you won before you called me after the game. The second I saw you calling, I was so deeply excited to share in that amazing moment with you. Since I have a part of me that is highly empathetic, my heart felt ready to burst out of my chest, and I had already stopped eating as those butterflies filled my stomach.

I picked up the phone, hit "accept," and energetically asked, "How did it go?" But I couldn't hear your response, so I looked at my phone to figure out if I had lost connection. By the time I put the phone back to my ear, I heard you on the other end, but no words were coming. Sometimes our brains are slow to process what we are hearing, and this was one of those moments. I was listening intently to figure out what was going on, and then finally, I heard noises that registered in my brain perfectly: you were crying. But not a subtle, soft cry. The sobbing on the other end of the line was a painful sob, the kind that makes you feel that person's pain from the deep core of their being.

I was in an instant panic as I tried to process why you were crying so painfully. All I could imagine is that you had been hurt playing and were being rushed to the hospital while I was stuck thousands of miles away, and my panicked helplessness was instantly overwhelming. What felt like minutes were probably seconds, but I finally heard your words through your sobs: "Daddy, he wouldn't play me. The coach wouldn't play me! I kept going over to the coach to ask to be put in, and he didn't do so until the very end. I only got to play one minute of the championship, and I'm so embarrassed and sad." My heart sank and blood rushed to my face as I felt the combination of your pain and deep anger toward your coach.

In that moment, all I could think about was the shock that a coach of seventh graders was more concerned about winning than creating a lifetime experience for everyone to be a part of the win. Yet, even in my moment of overflowing emotions, I was rational enough to attempt to give you the words you needed to hear: "Oh Morgan, the team couldn't have gotten to that spot without you. You have been a part of that team all season long, and you can hold your head high over that fact. The championship team includes you just as much as anyone else." But inside I felt very different. I felt your pain. I felt your anger. I felt your embarrassment, and I felt your emotions aimed at that coach who had created those harmful emotions.

The minute we hung up the phone, my thumbs took over before my brain could catch up. I didn't know how they could move that fast as I began to write an angry, feisty, "defending my daughter" letter to your coach. How dare he cause you that pain! Oh how I wish I would have been there to defend you, but he was going to hear about what I thought and felt. As a coach myself for over fifteen years, I had perspective that, when combined with my emotions, created as pointed of an e-mail as I possibly could write. I bet I damaged my phone that day as I wrote that e-mail with so much aggressive emotion. My emotions were swelling like a tidal wave, and I was about dramatically hit "send" when you called back and interrupted that chance. I answered the phone ready to feel more emotional fuel for my e-mail fire, but your words surprised me: "Daddy, I feel better now." I sat there on my hotel bed processing your words. You continued, "I figured out something as I processed what you told me. I'm Rudy! Just like Rudy (from the inspirational movie "Rudy" about a Notre Dame football player), I got to play the last one minute." All I could do is laugh, and although I still felt your pain and still do today, I hit delete on that angry e-mail and simply soaked up that moment with you.

Maybe that thinking is why I didn't want to create a blog for the entire world to see. Often when my unfiltered emotions take over, my words follow, and I know I would write something I would later regret. Words I wouldn't want you or other loved ones to read and words someone going through the same thing wouldn't need to read. Plus, I'm private, and I like to experience life with a small group of people instead of opening up my daily world for everyone to see. I value those who seek to be closest to me as I reach out right back to them. This amazing group of friends didn't reach out through a blog or tweet; they did so in a way that's honoring to me through each step of this journey. They used the right words and the perfect amount of effort. They didn't assume what I needed; rather, they asked and cared enough to truly listen and then honor.

By far, one of the best in this entire process was my friend Smiley. We call him Smiley for obvious reasons (plus we weren't too creative with nicknames). On the day I met him, his smile and kindness stood out in a sea of college freshmen. Smiley is as authentic and rare as they come, and the kind of person you are daily reminded about how blessed you are to have them in your life. For the two of you, I know there will be similar people who will come into your lives, and you will know instantly that you found a friend for life. Smiley was one of those friends. We met on the front porch of the Sigma Chi fraternity at the University of North Dakota on the very first time either of us visited the house.

Smiley and I both pledged Sigma Chi fraternity, and I was blessed by not only the chance to have him as a new friend, but 30+ others who formed a pledge class full of men of character and different temperaments, talents, and convictions. This group of men became lifelong friends, and they're a group I still keep in contact with today. Sigma Chi remains a true community for me where I feel the greatest sense of closeness and safety. But Smiley was different from others in my pledge class, and I've been able to have him as a best friend for more than twenty years now. I wonder who those friends will be for the two of you? Do you think you have met them yet or are they still on their way into your life? Do you have friends who ask you the hard and yet right questions and are willing to give you feedback?

Smiley was a mirror to me in how to share life with someone who is going through major life challenges. He would call me to check up on me almost daily. Sometimes I didn't have anything to say, so he would talk to me about something completely different and somehow make me feel normal. Although some days he was on the receiving end of an Abraham-Lincoln-type earful about where I was at emotionally, he remained steadfast. Even in the midst of the storms, when I looked around, he was right there with me. So it wasn't reading blogs and tweeting that helped my decision-making; rather, it was the chance to talk authentically to loved ones about all that I had been reading and thinking about. It was the chance to share with all of you, whom I deeply trust, and to hear your thoughts that were based on amazing listening and love.

All those conversations and research lead me to apply to the Mayo Clinic in Rochester, MN. The Mayo is yearly listed as one of the best hospitals in the world, and while I had never been there before, with them so close, I knew I had to at least try to see if they would meet with me. When I sent all of my information, MRIs, and medical records to them, it felt like I was applying to Harvard. I made sure everything was spelled correctly and my application was perfect. Two weeks later, I received my acceptance call, and my appointment with a team of doctors was set up for early November. I felt a sense of excitement about the possible guidance of these famous doctors, and of course the chance to learn something new.

Five

Double Reminder

My drive down to the Mayo Clinic from the Twin Cities was such an odd feeling. It was one of those days that my emotions were so jumbled, I couldn't separate out which emotion was which. On one hand, I was so deeply excited to talk to a team of doctors that were experts in their field and could help me sort through all I had read and learned. Yet I was also afraid of the unknowns, and I had fears of things not going as I hoped.

Lacking hope is a scary place to be, and I didn't want my mind to go there, so for part of the ride, I sang along to classic REM. Yet slowly, my anxious spirit began to internally erupt while my heart rate increased. Suddenly the fast beat of the drum that I loved so much in classic REM was pounding at the same speed as my heart. I quickly switched the dial to softer beat of classical music. I found myself slowly calming down and courageously switched back to REM, then classical, then REM . . . That pattern continued for the entire one-and-a-half-hour trip, my anxiety feeling like a roller-coaster ride the whole time.

The drive down to Rochester, MN ironically reminded me of my drive to Grand Forks, ND, to start school as a freshman at the University of North Dakota. UND is a campus of roughly 15,000 located in an adorable river town on the border of Minnesota and North Dakota, just hours away from Canada.

There is something special found in college towns like Grand Forks. They are rare gems in a sea of colleges and universities, and their alumni are still found wearing their alma mater's sweatshirts with pride years later. Since states like North Dakota don't have professional sports teams, the community embraces the university and follows their teams with a deep personal loyalty. When you are the main source of pride in town, that loyalty becomes a part of the community and students' DNA.

UND was a part of my mom's DNA, and she was the one who encouraged me to apply. My mom has always had this loving, kind way of encouraging and guiding me. I always felt like if I had said, "I want to be a garbage collector," she would have responded with, "You would be the most wonderful, perfect garbage collector!" She has a contagious joy and always wanted to help me succeed. She had attended UND, pledged Gamma Phi Beta sorority, and lived in the dorm right across the street from my freshman dorm. I remember her talking to me about how amazing the feel of the campus was and how special the people were that attended. Moms just know. She knew I would love UND, and she was right.

The minute my mom and I entered the UND campus, I needed to change the radio to classical music as the nerves began to swell in my stomach. I was about to get dropped off at my dorm and begin a new journey, and as an only child, this whole roommate idea was proving to be a bit more than I could process. I wish I could tell you two that I was strong and ready, but the reality is, I think the transition to college is hard. We will all tell you it's amazing, of course, and we'll talk about life-changing experiences and the new friends you're about to meet, but change can be hard, plain and simple. The minute my parents drove away, I felt the tears well in my eyes as I processed my new world. To add to my challenge, I was finally meeting my roommates for the first time.

My first roommate was Andy, a former tennis player and wrestler from Fargo. Andy was as nice as nice could be, yet he found his girlfriend in Fargo far more exciting than the Grand Forks on the weekends. Andy proved to be an easy roommate yet a distant one, while my other roommate Rob was from Grand Forks and decided he loved being in our room more than any other place on earth. For him, talking was far more challenging than sitting in silence and staring. The number of times I woke in the morning to him staring at me is more then any human should consider. Needless to say, going from my own room to one shared with two people drastically different from me was a huge challenge.

Thank goodness my friend Bret was across the hall. Bret also pledged Sigma Chi, and his faith, humor, and authenticity proved to be the perfect balance to my roommate situation. Plus he had an almost identical roommate scenario, and we counseled each other through our unique triple room situations. One of the best parts of my friendship with Bret was that his parents gave him a 1970s Jeep before he left Washington for North Dakota. He was one of my only friends that had a car on campus.

Thank goodness for that Jeep that allowed us to escape and head to the mall, restaurants, and any other place but our dorm rooms. Of course, that Jeep wasn't perfect: the 1975 original Jeep soft-top in below-zero temps made it a bit of a challenge to stay warm as we drove. One day as we drove past the Sigma Chi house on a perfect snowball-making day, one of our brothers threw a heavy, ice filled snowball in our direction. That frozen soft-top shattered like glass as that snowball landed in our laps inside the Jeep. Thank goodness for duct tape! Before we knew it, that window looked . . . well, it looked the best we could possibly have made it.

My world was changed the day I entered Grand Forks to attend UND, and driving to the Mayo Clinic felt equally life changing. I was about to meet a team of doctors that would have equally as powerful of an effect on me—hopefully in a positive way.

As I exited off the highway, I expected to see one giant hospital. Instead I was met by building after building, all owned by Mayo. I was blown away by the massiveness of the Mayo system and yet how each building was so unique and beautiful. Like the community of Grand Forks, I could see why the community of Rochester felt such a deep sense of pride about the Mayo system. I was also blessed by a beautiful sunny day and was soaking up the beauty around me when

I realized I was over two hours early. Of course my motto has always been. "If you are on time, you are late."

Not knowing what to do with all of that time, I decided to find a local breakfast nook that would provide some calming comfort food on an anxious day. I found an adorable, relaxing place just blocks away from my building, and when I first entered, I was the only customer in the restaurant. I ordered my favorite—eggs benedict and espresso coffee—and brought out the newspaper I had bought on my walk over. Ironically, I never once opened that paper. Right after I had been seated, a second set of customers was seated directly behind me, and they proved to be far more interesting than my paper. I couldn't see them since I had my back to them, but I heard the giggles of their children, and the more they giggled, the more I began to smile. Their tender voices provided the most beautiful, sweet, classical music to my soul. They created a heart-calming moment in which God reminds us of what's important in life.

While I was slowly eating, I could hear the parents talking to their children with such tenderness and love. They would ask perfect questions and wait with great patience while their children an-swered with long pauses, playful breaths, giggles, and words. Never once did I sense any bit of tension about how loud their kids were being or how long it was taking them to answer. Even when one of them dropped their sippy cup and some juice spilled out, never was there a raised voice or any sense of tension.

I sat reflecting on the love of parents and the joy of children. I at-tempted to eat slower, not wanting to miss a minute of the beautiful scene that was being played out directly behind me. Then I heard the kids talk about the joy of their hotel's swimming pool and the amazing french fries they had had the night before. Finally, I heard them compare their adventure to their home in Arizona. It sounded like they had been in Rochester for a bit of time, and I couldn't fully figure out their story until I got up to leave. I paid the server and stood up to see this wonderful family for the first time, and that's when I saw her. Their beautiful mom with her chemo-bald head sat looking as tired as tired could be, yet she had a loving, tender smile on her face. She knew what mattered, and it was the quality gift of time with her loved ones. I began my walk to my Mayo building with a calmed spirit and a sense of peace like I hadn't yet experienced in this process. So often I wait for burning bushes and for God to boldly proclaim what to do when, often, it's in the smallest of voices that He reveals himself to us. I hate when I'm too busy and miss those moments. Thank goodness for being early.

I walked into the giant Mayo campus building and was immediately met by volunteers who asked if I knew where I was going. I asked for the business desk and instead of someone simply pointing me there, she walked with me the entire way. Isn't it amazing how much those experiences matter to us? When I ask groups to talk about the worst customer experience they have ever had, every single person can come up with something. Those experiences stick with us, and we talk about them forever. For many, I think the great customer experiences can be more challenging to remember and talk about, but not for me. When I think of customer service and true customer engagement, I think of the Mayo. To this day, I've never been disappointed in my interaction with them.

After I checked in at the business center, that same volunteer, who had been waiting off to the side, then walked me up to my next appointment. With each step together, she would talk to me with her contagious joy about the building, community, and what she loved about her role. She wasn't just a trained volunteer going through a script in her mind; rather, she was living out the Mayo values, and her words and actions aligned perfectly. She dropped me at the line for my appointment and left to go impact another "customer." My next appointment's check-in was equally efficient, and within minutes I was sitting with my pager, waiting for my appointment to begin.

While I sat in the waiting area the size of a small gym filled with hundreds of seats, I noticed about ten to fifteen families sitting around me with their young children. Isn't it amazing how we can become so selfishly fixated on our own lives so much that we forget that others are going through similar challenges? Here I was just thirty minutes past my "breakfast values reminder," and yet I had to be reminded again that I wasn't the only one with a brain tumor or life challenges. I sat amongst children who were going through brain tumors and cancer, children who looked at me with giant smiles and bald heads, hearing aids, and even cranial scars. In one swift second, I was reminded for the second time that day of what's important in life and that even in the midst of challenges, I am blessed. I'm not sure why I needed two reminders that day, but I guess stress has a way of creating selfishness, and I was sure a walking example of that. A few minutes later, my Mayo pager went off, and I saw yet another smiling face: a nurse waiting at the doors to bring me back to my appointment.

She led me back to an examination room full of cherry cabinets and every electronic device possible. In just a matter of minutes, a team of doctors walked into the room along with a nurse practitioner and an assistant. Without missing a beat, they began to compare cranial surgery and Gamma Knife radiosurgery. Based on their words and research, I quickly shifted my interest to Gamma Knife as a possible next step. They were patient with me and allowed me to collect my thoughts and form my questions. Our meeting came to an end with my mind filled with a tremendous amount of information about Gamma Knife. I left with a great sense of what I had to do, but I needed to put those thoughts into words for my loved ones.

Six

The Kiss

My drive home felt completely different from my ride there. Maybe the stress of the unknown was better then the angst of the known. Suddenly, I had to take action and not just read and research. I was called to get out of my head and put plans and next steps into words for those around me. I had to think about what my life would look like post-decision and attempt to prepare for that future.

The reality is, this journey through life is meant to be shared with others, yet ironically, when we need people the most, we fall short at allowing them to love us and take the journey with us. While my professional life has been spent studying well-being and leadership, by no means do I think I know everything about human behavior. One area I want to research more is an observed human condition that challenges us to be vulnerable with the people around us when we are suffering. I was living out that undiagnosed human condition. I was left trying to find the balance between vulnerability and not wanting to create fear and anxiety in those around me. I felt that if I was too vulnerable, my words and actions would overwhelm those around me. Yet if I was too focused on couching everything with positive words and saying things like "Everything will be fine," I would lack authenticity. All these thoughts and emotions swirled around me like a storm daily.

If you two want to know how I actually felt, I was scared. I can say that today, but I couldn't then. Maybe I should have. Maybe that's what you needed to hear. I did the best I could to communicate during that time, but I know I fell short. In reality, I know you are learning much of what I was thinking and feeling at that time while reading this book. I'm sorry these words are so delayed. But I do want you to know that on my trip home from the Mayo, I knew what I needed to do. I had clarity and just needed to find the right way to communicate these next steps to you.

I wish I could tell you about the power of that conversation and how meaningful it was to all of us. But the sad reality is, I honestly don't remember much about that next steps conversation with your mom and you two. I know I wasn't able to articulate feeling vulnerable and scared. Instead, I focused on the facts. Why Gamma Knife felt like the clear option to me and what it would mean for work, life and our family. Normally, I would notice your responses to such an important conversation, but I was too numb to do so.

The words the Mayo doctors used provided me with a strong sense of peace about what my next steps should be, but not necessarily about their outcomes. But I figured I needed to focus on what I could control and not what I couldn't. I could control my emotional response, and I could attempt to prepare for my next steps. I called the Mayo back three days after my appointment and scheduled my Gamma Knife radiosurgery procedure. It was scheduled for December 23rd, 2011, and I immediately began my three week prep for surgery.

In Gamma Knife radiosurgery, specialized equipment focuses roughly 200 tiny beams of radiation on the tumor. To keep them from "missing" the tumor and damaging some important nerves, my head would be held down to the table by a cradle device that would be screwed into my head. From what I had read on blogs, the device was the most painful, scary part for the thousands that had gone through the same procedure. I also understood that after the procedure my head may be swollen and tender, and the implications of the Gamma Knife may impact my hearing, balance, facial nerves, and more.

One of the issues I struggled with was whether or not I would be able to continue my professional work post-procedure. With all of the things I needed to worry about, that should have probably been last on this list, but for some reason it was deeply at the forefront of my mind. As a speaker and consultant, I rely on my words and mind to impact clients, and I struggled with the thought of having facial drop or facial nerve damage. Isn't that vain? I fearfully wondered how people would look at me and how they would judge me. Maybe we all struggle with such thoughts, or maybe it was just me. But before I thought about whether or not I was being rational, I began to research other roles within my organization. Maybe I could coach leaders over the phone or create leadership curriculum instead of delivering it.

In the midst of my research, I was reminded of a story I had heard years ago about a young couple who had just gotten married when they found out challenging news of, you guessed it, a brain tumor. Unlike my options of radiation or surgery, the woman had to have her tumor surgically removed, and no matter how amazing doctors are, sometimes things happen in surgery that they so deeply want to avoid. While they were able to remove her tumor cleanly, they damaged her facial nerves during the procedure. As she began to wake from her surgery, she could see the caring looks of the staff and had an instant, gut feeling that there was more to their kind expressions and words than met the eye.

She calmly asked for a mirror and in that reflection saw her new face for the first time. The left side of her face, including the skin below her eyes and lips, was drooping and numb. When she tried to move her face, she found her movement limited to only one side. The tears began to flow as she processed what she was looking at. Her insecurity overtook her as she stared. But just then, her husband appeared and slowly bent down to kiss her for the first time post-surgery. She attempted to pucker her lips, but only half of her mouth moved, and the tears flowed even more. Her husband looked at her crooked lips and shifted his own to match them as best he could so their kiss would work perfectly. He smiled as he leaned up and said, "Look at that, still works perfectly."

Maybe, like her, my face would change, and maybe I would look different for the entire world to see, but my mind and the uniqueness of what I provide to people could still work perfectly. Ironically, perfection has never been something I sought—my C+ high school GPA was proof of that—so I concluded it wasn't the right time to worry about such things. My clients were simply going to get a new and improved Tom Matson. I told myself that a crooked face might even make me more fun and unique! Plus, I simply didn't know how I was going to respond to Gamma Knife since everyone's body reacts differently. It was going to take years for the scarring to take place, so I had no reason to worry about these things at that early stage. However, my emotions and thoughts were in overdrive. The emotions flowed so quickly that at any given second I could have a new thought, feeling of relief, fear, or anxiety. I wish I could say I was consistent, but that just wasn't true. I was a walking, talking example of inconsistency, and proud of it. I allowed myself to accept those feelings and thoughts as normal.

So Mr. Irrational Dad had his Gamma Knife surgery scheduled. I knew as much as I could understand. There was nothing more to research and nothing more to control. To fill that void, I began to clean the house perfectly on a daily basis. I grabbed ahold of anything I could control, and cleaning felt controllable. In addition, I think it was during this month that I spent the most amount of irrational money. Who could argue with anyone that claimed "brain tumor" for a purchase they were making? I don't think a day existed that Dave from UPS wasn't dropping off an Amazon package.

I was about to start a new chapter of life, one in which I was reminded so boldly that I'm not in control. If anyone wants to know what it's like to feel a lack of control, go through a medical procedure. You quickly understand the difference between control and hope. On this day, I simply had hope when it came to my medical care. My appointment was set, the house was clean, and my new sweater looked amazing. But preparing for Christmas sure felt different that year. "One day at a time," that's all I kept telling myself.

Seven

The Preview Before the Main Feature.

On December 22nd, my dad and I began our drive down to the Mayo Clinic for a day of pre-tests, or as I liked to call them, the preview before the main feature. I wanted my dad with me because I knew that he would talk about everything and anything besides the procedure. This is especially true about him when he is nervous and so the chance to talk about sports, weather and the news was a healthy escape from my emotions. Plus, I needed to know that the two of you would be safe at home with your mom.

The sun reflected off the snowy fields and provided a bright, beautiful day for us to enjoy as we drove. As I stared out the window, I reflected on the differences in scenery in the winter compared to summer. In my opinion, there is nothing quite as enchanting and peaceful as the summer fields in Minnesota. The miles and miles of grain-filled fields sway, calm and slow, in the wind. When you stand in front of them and feel the wind flowing through your hair, you deeply appreciate the sea of beauty in front of you. In those moments, I love to close my eyes and listen to the tranquil sounds of the swaying grain and soaking up the peace in that moment that provides calming medicine to my soul.

But for me, the winter fields of Minnesota feel very different. The snow-filled fields glisten as the sun reflects off the snow, and your eyes are drawn to objects we failed to see during those summer months rather than the swaying grain. It still amazes me how easy it is to miss the trees, wood fences and even the horses during the summer. Our eyes are so deeply drawn to the beauty of the fields that we miss the additional details that are right there in front of our eyes. But on this drive, I didn't miss them. I was caught off guard by the massiveness of the large oak trees that stood directly in the center of the fields in front of me. How could I have missed these large trees before? I found myself having a different emotional reaction to the trees than I did to the fields of summer. The large oak wasn't as relaxing as the calming fields; it felt out of place.

While I stared out the window reflecting on the awkwardness of the trees in front of me, my dad kept the cruise control at a very even 55 mph, and we slowly made our way down to Rochester. My attention shifted from the bold oaks in the fields to each car that passed. As each car sped by, my eyes locked with another passenger's. I attempted to guess their stories and wondered if they did the same with me. In my mind, every passenger that passed our car looked over to see the 6'4" fluffy-haired man in the Volvo driving next to them. Clearly none of them knew where I was going and what I was about to do, but I wondered if they, too, were on their way to Mayo. With the thousands that visit Mayo each year, it was certainly possible. I wasn't the only one anxiously making the drive down Highway 52. So the drive felt almost out-of-body. After trying for far too long, I attempted to accept my jumbled feelings and enjoy the ride.

I will be the first to admit that I don't have the greatest memory, yet oddly, I remember everything about that drive and day. I remember every billboard and every tree. I remember the smell of my dad's cologne and even what we were both wearing. I still have the flannel shirt I wore that day, even though I've only worn it a few times since. I guess that shirt is associated with those days for me, so I struggle to wear it and struggle to throw it away. But on a day I wanted to forget, my newfound ability to view this experience from an out-of-body lens allowed me to capture the memories perfectly in my mind.

We arrived midmorning for my first appointment, which was basically an hour-long conversation about my medial history, insurance, and questions about my upcoming procedure. I understand how valuable it is to double- and triple-check medical history forms, but I couldn't help to compare it to a job interview. Ironically, I felt that same interview nervousness we all get. In theory, I already had the "job," so I couldn't figure out why I was so nervous. I irrationally wondered if they would look at my recorded weight on the forms and question it after giving me a lookover. Maybe they would point out I had a few more grays and shouldn't label my hair color "brown."

I realized that my irrational thoughts were driving my nervousness, so I tried to take control by taking a long, deep breath and crossing my legs to appear relaxed. But no matter what I did, my nervousness continued. Suddenly, in between responding to her questions, I found myself throwing out nervous, awkward comments. They were the kind of statements you wanted to take back the moment you said them, yet I couldn't stop myself. "Hmm, that feels a bit personal for a first meeting," I would poorly joke. Of course, the nurse smiled and tilted her head to show care for me as she was trained to do. "Only among friends," I said later. The comments kept coming, and the more they flew out of my mouth, the more awkward I felt. *Get me out of here!* was all I kept thinking. Needless to say, I got through my interview and only regretted about 30% of our chat. Oh, and as I suspected, I got the "job" and was able to continue to my procedure. Lucky me.

My dad and I then had a break between appointments and went on a walk to find lunch in downtown Rochester. My phone was ringing off the hook with friends and family calling and texting to check up on me. Aren't we blessed to have those gifts in the form of a caring community that wants to make sure we are ok? I am convinced that I could have had a full room of people that would have been willing to sit with me and be there for me. Of course, that would have been my introverted nightmare. It would feel like opening up gifts on Christmas morning. For some reason, I always hated the attention of opening gifts at Christmas (the irony of being an only child), so I would wait until someone else began to open their gift and then quickly open mine at the same time. So it's safe to say that a waiting room full of family and friends staring at me lovingly wouldn't have felt relaxing to me. Plus, they wouldn't know each other, and that would just add to the awkwardness of the situation.

My Dad and I set off on the streets of Rochester to find our dream lunch spot. I've always loved the perfect sandwich, and we found one at a classic deli one block from Mayo. Isn't it interesting how food can be so perfectly linked to memories and experiences? I can remember those food-related moments like they were yesterday: trips to Smokin' Moe's in Winter Park Colorado, In-N-Out Burger in CA (which ruined my two-year run as a vegetarian), Aurelio's Pizza in Roseville, MN, and the Dock Café in Stillwater, MN. The perfect meal with the perfect memory attached to it. After just a few bites of the "Rainbow in Your Stomach" sandwich, our new deli was quickly added to my list of special places. In this case, it wasn't the conversation that made the meal so special, it's that it made me feel normal. All of those tests reminded me that there was a part of myself that was broken. Literally and figuratively, my brokenness was on my mind. But in that one precious moment in that deli, those thoughts were pushed away. I looked around the small space to see doctors, patients, and locals. None of us was talking about what was wrong or right in our lives; we were simply enjoying the comfort of a great meal in a peaceful space—another preview before the main feature.

With full stomachs, we walked back to the Mayo for my next round of appointments. We decided to use the "subway system" to get to our next appointment. The subway system at Mayo is a maze of underground tunnels that runs through a large portion of downtown Rochester. The system is perfect for the cold days of Minnesota, yet to newcomers, it can be confusing. At one point, we were lost. A staff member saw our panicked faces and came to our rescue. We would have been comfortable with him simply pointing us in the right direction, but he went above and beyond when he offered to walk there with us. We were amazed by the customer service and were even more blown away when we came to find out that this wasn't just a volunteer walking with us, it was the dean of the Mayo Medical School. Once again, we were shown the true definition of customer service and were reminded that at Mayo, all roles within the organization live the values of the Mayo Clinic.

Wouldn't it be a gift to the world if we could all do the same? If, when people thought about you, they thought about consistency with values and actions? That's what we felt at the Mayo when we experienced staff that lived their values authentically. I deeply hope that when people think of integrity, authenticity, and kindness, they think of you.

In addition, I hope when you think of those words, you have mentors, friends, and family members who show you what values in action look like. In order to live lives of integrity and authenticity, we need to open ourselves up and listen to the words of others. Yet we live in a culture that is often fearful of true feedback, but it's a gift, and that gift should always be loving and, at times, challenging. Feedback also gives you a chance to share what you want them to change, while also *helping* them do so. You should also know that it takes great courage to give others feedback and care enough to put that feedback into words when your emotions are healthy and you are not in an angry state of mind. We can never stop growing, and such communication provides the perfect chance to learn and develop into the leaders we are called to be. When we become such leaders, we take the time to walk scared patients to their next appointment in the subway system of Mayo. When we become such leaders, those scared patients write about you years later because of the impact you made on their life.

Here I am, years later, writing about the dean of the Medical School. Due to the dean's help, we arrived at my next appointment—my pre-procedure MRI—with a full five minutes to spare. This was my third MRI since they found my tumor, but at no point did they ever get easier for me. They reminded me of camp in 7th grade. I was in northern Minnesota at a camp owned by Young Life. At night we would gather as a large group to sing, watch funny skits, and hear amazing speakers. Our days were spent playing games, swimming, and, at the midpoint of the week, participating in the low ropes course, including "the tunnel." My 7th grade memory puts the tunnel at roughly one hundred yards and similar to the one in the movie "Shawshank Redemption" (though not as dirty). In reality, the tunnel was probably twenty yards tops and was a cement construction tube that was one part of the low ropes experience. Maybe it was about trust? Maybe it was a test of courage? I wondered if I had either one because I simply hated the experience. You squeezed your body into the cement tube and began to crawl as best you could. Seconds after entering the tunnel, all light was cut off, and instantly, tears of fear began to stream down my face. My friend Eric was in front of me, and I made him talk to me the entire time. After what felt forever but was probably just a few minutes, I was done with that tube and wanted to throw up. I was so worked up that I just couldn't calm down, even hours afterward. Even as I write about it, I relive that anxious feeling; it's the same one I had as they finalized my head brace and hit the button to slide my "tall glass of water" body into MRI tunnel.

While I have continued to struggle with MRIs, I have found small ways to make them better. First, I never open my eyes while in the machine. At the very point I know I'm about to be slid in, my eyes shut and don't open until I'm fully out of the machine. Second, before I even enter the room, I give myself something to think about. Doesn't that sound familiar, Ty? For as long as I can remember, you and I created that game before you go to bed. Your mom and I have always wanted to let you read for as long as possible before sleeping. In fact, that's why we always put you into bed so early: to develop a habit of reading. It was one of the best things we ever did. But even after all of those books, there were nights that reading couldn't calm you enough to fall asleep. (Unlike Morgan, who could fall asleep in two seconds in the middle of the Superbowl.) So I would give you a memory, place, or story to think about as you lay there, and it would relax you enough to allow you to sleep. I used that same game to help myself get through my MRI. I imagined myself on the beach, lying in the sun while listening to U2. My self-talk story calmed my spirits, and an hour or so later, I was slid out of the MRI machine, and my day of pre-tests was done. No more previews were in front of me, only the main feature. I anticipated it to be a movie that would be far too long and far too tiring.

That night, my dad and I found a cozy pizza shop and continued our conversations about life, the Fighting Sioux hockey team, and the weather. One thing I appreciated about the conversation was the way he snuck in caring questions about how I was feeling and how I was doing. My parents, like so many other parents, have always known how to calm me perfectly with the right questions at the right time. During this entire journey, our family—your mom, the two of you, my parents, and more—were great champions for me, and each of you played a needed role. Upon ending our dinner, we walked back to our hotel to attempt to sleep before our 4:00 a.m. wakeup.

I wish I could say I was so ready for my procedure that I slept like a baby. I wish I could tell you that I woke up the next day feeling a great sense of peace about what I was doing. I wish I could tell you that I felt confident. But I didn't. In fact, I'm not even sure why I had a hotel room because I didn't sleep a wink that night. I lay there wondering about what this new chapter in my life would feel like. I lay there fearful of how the next day was going to impact me and if I was going to ever be the same Tom again. The reality is, I knew the answer: I wasn't. I was simply going to trust the process and take it one day at a time. Cleary there was no reason to have set my alarm, and the next day when I saw my dad, I realized he hadn't slept a wink either. We began the slow drive over to the hospital to take the next step together. Snow was falling slowly, and the streets were quiet. It was time for the main event.

Eight

Mountain Climbing

The abandoned streets of Rochester were breathtaking at 5:00 a.m. The snow was slowly falling, and the Christmas lights still flickered their brightness as they slowly swayed in the wind. Neither of us could find the right words to say at such an ungodly hour on such a rare day, so we simply stared out the windows and soaked up the beauty around us. It was one of those days that time stopped, and I still remember every smell, detail, and emotion. We've all had days like that. For example, I could tell you exactly where I was when President Reagan was shot, when the shuttle *Challenger* exploded, when the September 11th attacks occurred. Millions share some of our life experiences, while some are shared with a select few, but they all are equally powerful.

Our drive came to an end as we slowly pulled into the parking lot roughly a half hour early. I figured it couldn't hurt to be first. I felt like the Griswolds pulling into the parking lot of Walley World as I looked around and realized we were the only car there. We walked through the snow, creating a path that hundreds others would take that same day. Though I would never get to talk to any of them, I knew that many others would each experience their own life-slowing moments throughout those Mayo buildings, each equally as powerful as the next.

That's something that's always bugged me throughout my life. There are certain people who think their lives are worse than others', that they have been dealt a worse hand in life. The reality is, we all have our "thing" that we have to deal with during our lives. Some find out what it is early in their lives, like my wonderful friends who were born with Down Syndrome, while others discover it later in life. But we all have our challenges. Life has highs and lows; that's what life is. On that day that I had to deal with my "thing," I knew others were too. Maybe that perspective is why I sought out blogs and online communities early in my diagnosis. While I never wrote anything, I read thousands of thoughts and feelings about others' journeys. Each of us approaches life in a different way, and each of us views life through our own lens. None better, none worse. So I've learned that each of our stories makes us powerful humans, and I loved learning from everyone who shared their story.

The differences in our life stories and our responses to life come down to how we persevere. Since we all have our "stuff" to deal with, it's not the "stuff" that defines us. Rather, it comes down to how we respond to it. I truly believe that's a choice we can make. I could choose to let this tumor define who I am, or I could embrace it and not let it control me. In fact, a basic mindset I share with the tennis players on my team is that during a match, they will have great points and bad points, just like their opponent. The difference comes down to how they respond emotionally to both. Will they waste emotional energy in good times and bad, or will they find a way to stay even keeled?

I could write about our response to life for the majority of this book, but I think it's easier to let these words, attributed to Reinhold Niebuhr, sum it up perfectly: "God grant me the serenity to accept the things I cannot change; courage to change the things I can; and wisdom to know the difference." Our lens on life is ours and ours alone, and we can choose to be paralyzed by life, or we can choose to climb that mountain and embrace all the richness that life offers us.

When I slowly opened the door to the hospital, my own climb up the mountain was beginning for the day. I simply attempted to take on the day's adventure with a courageous mindset. Upon entering the waiting area, we guessed which door my name would be called from and found seats in that area. At that time in the morning, the waiting room was filled with the cleaning staff shining the floors, plus my dad and I. But one at a time, more people walked in, and as each person entered, I found myself becoming more and more uptight. I wanted to smile at everyone and say, "You do realize I was the first one here," but I didn't want to add greater tension to what was obviously a stressful situation to begin with for all of us. In reality, I just wanted my day over with. There was nothing more to it. No one wakes up hoping to have their brain zapped with radiation. The sooner I could get up this mountain, the better off I would be.

Thirty minutes later, they called my name, and I got up to continue up the mountain. Upon walking through the doors, the nurse asked the same questions I would be asked over and over all day long: name, social security number, birthday. Of course, she was kind and asked how my day was going. An ironic question for 5:30 a.m. on the day I'm about to have my brain radiated.

"Oh I guess I could think of better days," I responded, and she simply smiled. We rode the elevator in silence, and she brought me to the changing room and instructed me to change into my gown and place my personal items in the portable locker.

While I changed out of my clothes in the "locker room," I felt my emotions swell up. Somehow changing out of my clothes and into that gown felt symbolic of another change I was about to go through. From *my* clothes and *my* control to *their* clothes and *their* controlled world. I guess it was an understatement to say I was having control issues and my emotions weren't happy with it. I tried everything in my power to calm myself and my breathing, but in reality, my response was healthy and human. Plus, I clearly needed to spend my emotional energy on more important things that day. So I walked out of the room with my awkward gown on, wearing my too-small socks with the rubber bottoms, and finally, with my red eyes. My nurse tilted her head empathetically and smiled before leading me to a larger room with four or five spaces separated by curtains.

We walked into the curtained area that would store my locker, and I sat on the gurney that would be my home for the next six hours. Then I remember the nurse looking me straight in the eyes and saying, "We're going to do this day together. I'm going to be with you each step of the way."

I found such great comfort in those words that I became my normal, playful, smart-alecky self. "Well not *every* step of the way," I joked, and we laughed together. She was as playful as I was, and I enjoyed our banter back and forth while she took my vitals and asked me, yet again, for my name, social security number, and birthday.

My doctor that day is one of the world experts in brain tumors, and I trusted him fully with my health and well-being. I was so thankful to be at the Mayo and so thankful he was my doctor. His expertise and credentials provided peace to balance my anxiousness, but one thing I knew he would not provide was humor. To put it bluntly, he just wasn't funny in any way. When he walked into the room, he set the emotional room temperature. I had noticed his lack of humor during my first appointment with him, and I found him to be the same way on that early morning as well.

But something inside me decided to make him my challenge for the day. I guess it was due to my need to control anything on a day I felt so powerless. So when he exited my curtained space to check on the others in the room, I shared my goal for the day with my new favorite nurse. While she surely loved my playful, humorous side, she prepared me to not be caught off guard when he didn't find me as entertaining as the rest of the team did. Notice she didn't say *if* but *when*. But I looked her in the eyes and said boldly, "I'm going to make him laugh today. Not just a smile, but a pure laugh." She tilted smiled, and nonverbally communicated, "Yeah, good luck." But I was determined.

As the day went on, every single time I was left alone with my thoughts for even a few minutes, my heart instantly beat out of my chest. So to calm myself, I tried to look around and see who else was in my new, curtained home. I quietly tried to listen to the others conversations, and it finally dawned on me that I wasn't the only one there to receive Gamma Knife radiosurgery. Somehow it hadn't registered with me that they would have more than one procedure per day.

I heard one voice that sounded older than I, and I heard what I thought was a younger woman's voice as well. Finally, I heard another man's voice that I thought sounded of similar age. I wanted to ask all of them, "What are you in for?" but knew I would never have the chance to talk to them. But they were real people feeling the same fear, the same anxiousness as they started a new mountain journey with me. To this day, I wish I could have exchanged personal information with them and been able to know how they've been doing post-procedure.

But life doesn't always allow that. Sometimes we are called to fend for ourselves on the mountain. I think that's one reason so many people die at high altitudes while climbing Mount Everest. When climbers come upon other climbing parties above the Death Zone (26,000 feet), they are simply fending for their own lives and trying to survive. Sadly, even if another party's climbers are dying, they will often pass them by without saying a word while remaining focused on their own lives and goals. But this wasn't Everest, and my morals remained steadfast as I sat waiting and thinking about others' journeys. I knew that in that room there were anxious, real people with worried families and friends, just like me. We were in this climb together.

Though I wished for a chance to get to know them, I began my own solo climb up the mountain, and I wanted to be first to the summit. In my mind, the first one into the Gamma Knife room is the first one out, and the first one done is the first to go home. I sat there strategizing how I could be first, and I concluded the easiest patient would go first. They would get the easiest procedure and patient out of the way and save the time for more challenging patients. So I told myself to not complain about anything and to not let anything get in my way of winning this painful sprint to the summit.

Minutes later, my doctor and his intern walked into my curtained space to start the process of prepping me for the procedure. In with them came the "crown" I would wear for the day: my head brace. I know that's not the medical term for it, but I loved referring to it as a crown instead of a brace. Although, to be honest, it looks nothing like a crown, so I'm not sure why I called it that. This was the first time I had actually seen it in person, and it looked as miserable as I imagined. It was comprised of four metal bars roughly six inches in length that would extend down to around my chin. Around my chin, there was a metal bar that would be attached to the table during the radiosurgery to keep my head from moving. At the top of each of the four bars were spaces for large metal screws that would be screwed into my cranium to hold everything perfectly in place. My eyes darted between each component of my crown. Everyone was talking, but I wasn't hearing a thing.

I finally began to focus on my doctor's words and understood that both he and the intern would be giving me large shots of a numbing solution to help prepare me for the screws. Now I don't know about you, but I hate shots, and these were big needles. However, I figured if there were any day to embrace the benefits of a shot, this would be it because gosh those screws looked thick. So they each picked up the syringe and simultaneously pierced my skin to inject the numbing solution into my forehead. The first two spots were roughly an inch above my eyebrows, and when they finished there, they did the same thing at the same level on the back of my head. We sat there for few minutes in silence, waiting for the numbing solution to do its job. It burned a bit, and my goal to make the doctor laugh was the last thing on my mind. After enough time had passed, they tested the sensitivity on my forehead, but I could still feel their touch, so they added more numbing solution to that area. After a few minutes, I felt ready enough to let them try again.

They slid the "crown" over my head, and I became a bit anxious and claustrophobic as the frame was slid over my large cranium, slightly squishing my nose on the way down my face. I realize I have a big head, like an orange on a toothpick, but this frame would feel overwhelming to anyone. Once they had my crown in place, they prepped the screws to be drilled into the holes. I appreciated having two people to screw at the same time to create a counter pressure on my skull. While my doctor screwed in the front right screw, his intern screwed in the back left one. I felt the warm blood streaming down my face, but I couldn't feel much more than that, so I guessed the numbing injections were working.

For some reason, I had been more afraid of those screws than the radiation itself. How could you not think of Frankenstein as you hear it described? In fact, that's exactly what I was imagining as they finished screwing. They screwed in the last two screws, and while the front one was once again painless, the back right one wasn't painful by any means, but it was uncomfortable. However, in that moment I decided that I had already slowed their process once when I made them add more numbing solution, and if I did so again, they may need to go onto another patient first. So I said nothing. I figured I could deal with some discomfort for a while. Shortly after, all the screws were in place and my "crown" was firmly on my head.

The two doctors went on to repeat the same process with the other three patients while I adjusted to the new addition to my body. I could feel the pressure of the screws on my head like a deep, consistent force against my skull. Besides that one back screw and the heaviness of the frame, I was adjusting to this new feeling. The pressure did take time to get used to, though. No matter how much I read about it and no matter how much they told me, I still had an irrational fear that the pressure from these screws would cause my head to crack. I tried to move slowly and methodically so there was no additional pressure on the screws themselves. Despite my intentional lack of movement, it continued to feel like the largest pressure headache I have ever experienced. I concluded that it wasn't going away until those screws were removed, so I prepared myself for the rest of the day with that nasty headache and the continued journey up the mountain.

While the two doctors finished up prepping the other patients, I got to leave my curtained home and was wheeled away to receive a more detailed MRI and CT scan. Obviously, when dealing with such strong doses of radiation, not moving, even a fraction of an inch, is essential. While I had had an MRI the day before, this new MRI and CT scan were to take place with my crown firmly locked into place so they could align the Gamma Knife machine perfectly. The area was a considerable distance from my room, and it took quite a bit of time to get there. However, it wasn't the distance that stuck out in my mind as I was wheeled through the hallways. Rather, it was the looks on the faces of the people we passed.

As we approached people in the hallway, I would watch their eyes from a distance as they looked at me and attempted to understand what was on my head. Yet as we got closer to them, they would quickly shift their eyes away in an attempt to make me feel like they hadn't been staring at me. Ironically, I knew exactly what they were doing because I know I've done the same. It may have been a homeless person, someone with a facial deformation, or just someone different from me. But I know I've stared and then attempted to hide it, and I now know exactly how that feels.

It clearly bugged me, so I stared back at them so they knew I had seen them. But after a while, I guess I became numb to their looks. Rather than focusing on them, I went back into my mind and processed what I might look like after the procedure. I wondered if such stares would be more prevalent in my future due to a shift in my appearance. I knew this process would create a new journey for my life, but seeing people view me as physically different wasn't something I was used to. It certainly made me more sensitive to and more aware of my own reactions to people. I just wish those who were staring at me would have kept looking, and then smiled and said hi. I wish they would have acknowledged me as a human being first and foremost. Sometimes life forces us to learn new lessons even before we're ready to learn them. Here I was, about to have my brain zapped, and instead of thinking about that, I was thinking about how I interact in this world with those who are different from me. Before I could have any more time to think, we arrived at the area for both of the machines.

I was wheeled in, and my eyes quickly shifted to that MRI machine that was in the middle of the large room. My pulse increased. MRIs were hard enough for me, but to add to the tension of this particular MRI, I needed to have an additional helmet-type object placed over my crown. They taught me that the helmet, as I referred to it, was actually called a stereotactic frame. The frame has a grid on it that is a used to more precisely pinpoint the specific tumor location and dimensions. While that was all very interesting, I just knew they had to slide a boxed frame over my crown before my MRI. However, they had a problem: my darn big head.

My head was so big, it wouldn't fit into any of the frames they had in the room, or in that part of the hospital. I was surrounded by a group of five technicians and nurses brainstorming how to get the frame over the crown on my head. They attempted over and over to use the largest size they had in the room, but each time, my nose was pushed all the way in, so I was left to breathe through my mouth only. It was so tight and close to my face that I could even feel my long eyelashes brushing against it. Having another MRI was stressful enough, but the need to be a mouth breather to get it done was far above my comfort level.

My stress level elevated to a new high when I saw my doctor walk into the room, ready to go, and I was still sitting there, not set for my MRI. His schedule was tight that day, and any delay would either throw off the other procedures he had scheduled or my spot in the lineup. He immediately asked what was wrong and they explained that they had a frame issue. So here was my chance, my chance to win my bet with my nurse. Without missing a beat I blurted, "None of them want to say it, but my head is so big we don't have a frame that can fit over this melon. I'm more like a watermelon then a cantaloupe. We're talking the size of Jupiter compared to our moon."

My loud interruption forced the group into silence, and they all slowly turned their heads to watch the doctor's response. My doctor paused as he processed my words, and then it came, like a small, growing flame that suddenly bursts into a raging fire. It was a magical sound: the most beautiful laugh you have ever heard. It was not just a small courtesy laugh either; it was a good, hard belly laugh. The room joined in, and we all laughed together. Oh, how a hard laugh releases tension and helps remove stress. We all relaxed together, the doctor called for the largest frame they had from a different area of the hospital, and we waited for it to arrive together.

Roughly ten minutes later, the frame arrived and was slide down over my crown. While it still touched the tip of my nose (maybe I have a big nose, too), it was comfortable enough to allow me to complete my scans. I was then taken back to my curtained home to "rest" while the doctors, assisted by a computer, mapped out the plan of attack. Joining my doctor was a physics oncologist who worked with the team to pinpoint the exact measurements and head positioning needed to attack my tumor perfectly.

That attention to detail provided such important relief. When you are about to be shot by radiation beams over 200 times, you don't want them to miss. While I sat there waiting for them, my nurse smiled and softly said, "You win."

We smiled together, and I was reminded how thankful I was for angels that appear to us on such days. Typically we don't see them again, yet they are the right person at the right point in our lives, and they are gifts. I hope I can be such a person, and I hope both of you kids can as well. I also hope I get to meet more of these angels throughout my lifetime.

I think that's why almost every expedition up Everest had a Sherpa with them. That comforting Sherpa was like a guide or mentor. They are known for their contagious, joyful smiles and calming demeanors. As I was on my mountain-climbing adventure that day, I had my own Sherpa in the form of my loving and caring nurse. Just like a Sherpa, her warm smile calmed my spirit, and her words did the same. I couldn't have done that day without her, and I wish I could go back and share that with her today.

I had waited roughly an hour when she came back in and said, "It's time." We began the journey to the summit of the Gamma Knife room together. My trusty guide leading me and staying with me just as she has promised. They say the last climb to the summit is the most challenging, and I sure understood that, as I was about to feel the same challenge. But I had to get through it. I had to see my family again and celebrate Christmas, which was just days away. She pushed me down to the room in silence. The summit was within my view.

Nine

The Day was Finally Here

Smells have always stood out to me and gone hand-in-hand with instant flashback memories. When I think of playing soccer as a child, I think of the smell of freshly cut grass. When I think of hockey, I think of the smell of the sweat-soaked equipment, and finally, when I think of tennis, I think of the smell of a can of brand new tennis balls. The minute I smell those things, I am instantly brought back to those moments on the field, ice, or court.

Smells stir up different memories for each of us. To this day, when I think of the dentist, I think about gagging to the smell and feel of getting my teeth fixed. I say, "fixed" because besides concussions and a brain tumor, the only other time I've "broken" anything, forced me to bond with dentists far too much over my young life. Of course, just like this journey started with a hockey adventure, my previous tooth break started with an adventure as well.

Growing up, I had the opportunity to share my birthday with my best childhood friend, Eric (and later in life, with your mom). Our birthdays were just a week apart, so oftentimes our birthday parties would be planned together. Most years we went to Valleyfair, a local amusement park, but one year, we scrapped that plan. The reality is, even the best plans need to be adjusted at times. In this case, it was our gifts that created the opportunity.

There was something fun about opening up our gifts on the same day, and yet the older we got, the more it shifted from being fun to being a contest. I had been able to open up a few smaller gifts on my actual birthday even though our shared party was roughly a week later. We had invited all of our friends (each other) and were set for a day of roller coasters, carnival games, and pronto pups. But when I walked into the living room on my birthday and saw the magic that was in front of me, I knew that plan was going to change. There it was, reflecting in the sunlight of our front window: a brand new bike. Now it wasn't just any bike; it was magical and beautiful. The orange paint glistened in the living room lights, and that banana seat . . . wow! That seat could hold hundreds of my closest friends. I also loved those giant curved handlebars and the orange tassels. I was staring at the most perfect bike known to man. Even more exciting, it was a Huffy.

After sitting on my bike in the living room for a few minutes, I carefully pedaled it over to the phone and called Eric right away. "No bike riding in the house!" I heard my parents yell, but I had to tell him about my amazing new gift! Sometimes I stutter when I get excited, and this was no exception. So here I was, stuttering and trying to get the perfect words of excitement out, but before I could, Eric jumped in with his words. "Tom, I got the greatest gift ever today! I got a bike, and not just any bike: I got the new Huffy with the shock on the front!" All of which was communicated in roughly one second.

I was quiet on the phone as I processed his words and shared back that I, too, got a Huffy, but I did so with a bit less excitement than I had had seconds before. My model was a bit older and more out-dated than the new model Eric had received. Eric's new bike had a thick metal shock on the front that caused the wheel to move with any bumps. Suddenly, I was having Toughskin flashbacks and feeling behind the times again. Before we had hung up the call, matching words came out of our mouths about the changes in store for our party. No longer were we going to Valleyfair. We were going to Hawks Jump.

Hawks Jump was *the* place to go for dirt bikers. It was where all the cool kids biked. Hawks was a giant dirt crater full of huge jumps with pits behind them. In the winter, it was our sledding dream, and in the summer, it was our biking fantasy. A friend's dad took care of the hill, and he would extend hoses from their house to spray it down and get the perfect jumps and smooth, packed surface.

When we arrived, the place was already packed full of bikers fly-ing off the jumps while kicking out their back tires. As we looked around, we saw others jumping up and down on pedals attached to their back wheel, and even more doing just about every other bike trick known to man. It dawned on my young mind that maybe we should have practiced before jumping right into the Everest of dirt biking, but before we could turn around, a bunch of them biked over to us. "You here for the first time?" they asked.

"Yes, we just got new bikes for our birthdays!" Clearly no one cared, and no one smiled.

"Well if you're here for the first time, you need to do Suicide," and they pointed to the largest hill with the biggest jump. Now I don't know about you, but that word didn't make it sound like the safest of hills, and anyone with any bit of common sense would have passed. But sometimes peer pressure gets the best of us in 5th grade, so before I had the time to put any thoughts into words, I heard Eric volunteer to go first.

Eric and I began the long ride up Suicide. In fact, we weren't even able to make it to the top because it was so big. We had to get off our bikes and walk the rest of the way up. "We're saving up our energy," I yelled over my shoulder.

When we finally got to the summit, we pointed Eric's bike in the right direction of the giant jump. He got all set on his bike, and I got behind him and gave him the biggest running push possible. I watched Eric's mullet flying in the wind with him biking as hard and fast as he could possibly bike. His new, fancy bike was made for moments like this, and I could imagine him soaring over that jump and the pit behind it.

He was ten feet away from the jump, and I could feel the excitement swell in my throat. BAM! He hit that jump with as much momentum as a rocket, but instead of flying off that jump like I had pictured, he was pulled straight back to earth and into the far sidewall of that pit. Those new shocks of his must have weighed one hundred pounds because no matter how hard he pulled up on those handlebars, the weight of those shocks kept him planted to the ground. Not only that, but that firm dirt was like a brick wall, and it caused his bike to come to an immediate halt with such strong force that his new seat snapped in half. Eric painfully and awkwardly landed on the middle bar of his bike. He sat on that bar, frozen in time, until he slowly tipped over.

I ran down the hill as fast as I could (which was, again, the speed of a turtle) and didn't know what to do. There was Eric, sitting in the pit, his wheel bent under his bike and his broken seat lying right next to him. I picked up the seat and handed it to him, reminding him that my dad had duct tape and we could fix it. We got ready to leave, and Eric began gingerly walking home with me when the group stopped us once again. "Matson, your friend may have tried to bike Suicide, but if you ever want to come back here again, you have to try, too. We've all done it, and now it's your turn."

Despite my love of words, nothing came out of my mouth. Before I had a chance to respond, it dawned on my 5th grade mind that maybe Eric didn't make it over that jump because he needed a banana seat and more weight on the back of the bike to create even greater momentum. So I began my walk up the hill with Eric in tow, ready to hop on my banana seat with me to make the long trek down together. Surely this was going to be perfect.

I put Eric on the back of the banana seat, and it felt like he was sitting over a mile away when I looked back. He was still holding the half of his seat that had snapped off. But I was ready to go, so I pushed off and began biking as fast as possible. My hair was flying in the wind, and I could hear Eric slightly spitting as my hair flew back into his face and mouth. My hockey haircut may have looked amazing under a helmet, but under these conditions, Eric wasn't a fan. I could see the jump approaching and started to giggle with excitement as I imagined soaring off of that jump. Yet when we hit the jump, instead of flying off of it, it felt more like a car going slowly over a speed bump. In fact, my two wheels never left the ground due to all the weight on that bike. Not only that, when we hit the back of the pit, Eric's weight came crashing into me, causing my smiling, giggling face to shoot forward. The next thing I knew, my teeth were hitting those tall, curved handlebars at full steam and with such force that I flew backwards, knocking Eric off the bike.

My bike came to a crashing halt, and as I lay there, I could feel the wind whipping into my mouth. I slowly reached up to find my two front teeth completely cracked open. A new pyramid shape sat between what used to be my front teeth. I began a failed mad scramble to find the missing pieces on the ground, thinking that if I found them, I could simply put them back in. I searched for a while, and then in a panic, I got on my bike and began the mad ride home, only looking back once to see Eric still lying in the pit with his broken seat in hand. "Tom?" he yelled, but I didn't listen.

I came bursting through the doors of my house with tears streaming down my face, and my mom couldn't understand what happened till I opened my mouth. Within seconds, we were on our way to the dentist, a place where I would spend countless hours over my lifetime attempting to fix and re-fix those broken teeth. For some reason, I had a hard time not re-breaking them, from the time I bit through the stick while eating a cheese-on-a-stick, to the time they were stuck in my mouth guard during a hockey game. But each and every time, I was brought back to the dentist and reminded of that smell. I had smelled it on the day of that first fateful biking accident, and I smelled it each and every time after. That smell was created by a combo of smoking, drilled teeth and dental toothpaste; they came together to create that nightmare stench. Each and every time I smell it, my stomach becomes instantly upset. I still take TUMS before I get my teeth cleaned due to my emotional reaction to the smell. To this day, the instant I smell that stench, I'm anxious and fearful, and I flash back to my broken teeth.

While breaking my teeth wasn't at the same level of severity as my Gamma Knife procedure, the smell of the hospital that day sure is equally connected to my emotional response forever. The second I was wheeled into the giant, white Gamma Knife room, that clean, disinfected smell combined with an electrical smell filled my nostrils. Soon it was equally etched in my memory. But it wasn't just the smell that stood out to me. The bigness of the machine and the room combined with a sterile feel to make the room void of emotions. Like a dementor from *Harry Potter* was in the room sucking the joy out of the room.

On the far side of the room were thick windows to allow the staff to look in. The room felt as overwhelming as the task at hand, and I began to wrap my mind around the bigness of the situation. This wasn't just a bike trip down Suicide at Hawks Jump. It was a new chapter in a book I had been forced to read. Biking was an option while this was a requirement, and I had to remind myself to take deep breaths to collect myself. Plus those darn windows made me feel like some sort of experiment, an observed species, and it just felt lonely. I guess my positive emotions were indeed being slowly sucked out of me.

While I was attempting to calm myself, the staff in the room was preparing the last-minute details, and they moved me to the "couch," as they called it. Now, this was unlike any couch I have ever sat on, and if it was indeed a couch, it certainly wasn't a very comfy one. I sat on what felt like an inch of foam, and then they told me to lie down. Since I don't wear dresses on a regular basis, it was a bit awkward as I attempted to lie back without exposing too much of myself under the gown. Once I had adjusted my gown and gotten as comfortable as possible, they began to attach my head frame to the table. While it wasn't a bad experience by any means, it did feel a bit uncomfortable as they arranged my head before locking it down.

When your head is held down by a metal frame screwed into your skull, it's an understatement to say that you feel anxious. It becomes an internal battle of will as you attempt not to panic. Suddenly I had never wanted to look around so much in all my life. But I was given just one view in that moment: up. I could look straight up and straight up only. To add to the discomfort, one of the screws in the back of my head was being pressured as it lay against the couch. The staff, sensing my discomfort, did their best to calm me and even put a blanket over me before leaving the room. But the second they shut the door, I heard nothing but the sound of my own breathing. I waited in silence for the music they had promised to begin. Since it was December 23rd, they had asked if I wanted to listen to holiday music during my procedure. For some reason that sounded perfectly comforting, and I agreed to their choice of music. But it didn't come. The longer I went without it, the more I hated to hear my breathing, and I closed my eyes and took slow, deep breaths to calm my spirit.

While they finished up their last computer details for the Gamma Knife machine in the other room, I tried to focus my thoughts on the right things. I attempted to think about the celebrations of my life and what I was most thankful for, and my breathing began to slow until I heard the doors to the machine opening behind me. They were roughly four feet across, and once they were open, my couch slid me back into the half-moon crater of the Gamma Knife machine. I was maybe two or three feet into the machine, and I was thankful to still be able to see the light of the room. In fact, it felt far less claustrophobic then an MRI machine, but by no means was it any more comfortable emotionally or physically. I was ready for them to begin so I could get this moment over with. I thought, *it could never get worse than this.* Never ever say that phrase, and never ever think it. For in that moment, the holiday music started.

When I think of holiday music, I think of "Silent Night" and "Rudolph the Red-Nosed Reindeer." So when they told me about the music, I imagined it as a relaxing distraction I could sing along with. While I don't have the best voice, in that particular moment, I simply didn't care about their critique of my singing. I wanted to test the acoustics in that room and see if sound would truly bounce around in there as much as I thought it could. Sadly, the second the music started, my concert dreams were thrown out the window, for the music blared through the speakers was like no holiday music I have ever heard. There's no other way to say it: it was horrible. Just horrible. Even though I heard the word "Christmas" in the songs, it sounded like some locals had made up new holiday music and recorded it at home. I now had a second reason to want to get out of that room: cruel and unusual punishment in the form of bad holiday music.

I was briefly relieved from the pain when my doctor, who sat behind me in the glass room, briefly interrupted the music. He told me that they were about to begin, and he described how the couch will slowly move up and down and side to side to place me into the right position for each radiation treatment. The painful music came back on, the process began, and I shut my eyes. In this irrational moment, I somehow wondered if the radiation was bad for my eyes, and I thought shutting them was the easiest way to protect them.

I felt the couch begin to move and heard the clicking of the machine behind me, and in that moment, I knew a new chapter of life was beginning. I prayed, and I took deep breaths and again thought about more things I am thankful for. I thought about my friends and family and thought about the many of you reading this book today, and I was thankful for all of you. In fact, thinking about all of you made me softly cry.

So many of you chose to take this journey with me, and I could feel you in that moment. I also thought about growing up and the rocket park that I so deeply loved, and I thought about Christmas memories as well. I could imagine the details of dinners with the Christiansen's, twice-baked potatoes, opening one gift on Christmas Eve, sandbag candles lining the streets, and my favorite gifts through the years. Sometimes in life, our mind wants to run to dark places, but we need to stop it before it goes down that road. My memories of all of you got me through that moment, and I was so thankful to celebrate those of you I have known for years and those of you I have yet to meet.

The longer I lay there, the more the back of my head hurt. I hated the feel of that one screw uncomfortably pushing against my head, and not only that, I began to get a squirmy body feeling. My legs felt restless, and the more I wanted to move, the more I had to remind myself to stay completely still. I clearly didn't want them to miss. The couch continued to move, and I counted to sixty over and over in my head.

I had a rough idea of how long I was going to be in there, and my memories were beginning to run low as I became more un-comfortable. I was counting down in my head to get through the process. In fact, I was beginning to feel the panic of being trapped when I finally heard it: a voice of reassurance that I was done and they were on their way to detach my head from the table. It felt like forever, but after they slid my couch out of place and shut the doors to the machine, two people appeared and began to detach my frame from the couch. As they did, I quietly said, "I did it." I *had* done it. I had conquered my fears. I had climbed my Everest. My fearful tears shifted to relieved tears and flowed down my cheeks as I repeated those words out loud, over and over. After all those months of built up anxiety and feeling so deeply powerless, my emotions flowed in that moment, and I sobbed deeply.

They put their arms around me and walked me back over to my portable bed, and I sat down and then lay back. I felt a bit dizzy and wasn't sure if it was due to the emotions or the Gamma Knife. I then made the trip back upstairs with my favorite nurse with me the entire way. I loved the comfort of having her there with me, so I let my emotions flow, and the tears streamed down my cheeks. She would stop along the way and put her hand upon my shoulder, and I would cry more. When we were finally back on our floor, she pushed my bed into a different space from where I had spent the morning. I was in a room all to myself, and inside was my locker with my clothes. Seeing that locker reminded me that I was coming to the end of my mountain climbing for the day, and I was ready. I was exhausted physically and even more so emotionally.

After lying there for a bit, I was finally able to sit up. When I did, my angel nurse and one of her coworkers did what I had been dreaming of all day: they unscrewed my crown, and I was free. I again felt the blood trickling down, and she quickly put bandages on my two front wounds and then wrapped a giant role of gauze around my entire head.

We sat talking for a bit when they finally asked if I felt well enough to get dressed. "Of course," I said, even though I wasn't. Yet I knew that getting dressed was another step toward my finish line. So they left the room and waited in the hallway while I slowly got on the same clothes I had worn to the hospital earlier that day. It felt like I had been there for days, and as I was buttoning up that shirt I felt the tears stream down my face again. What a day. What a scary, exhausting day. I took a deep breath and wiped those tears away and told them they could come back in the room.

They then spoke the words that put the end of my day within view: "If you can walk around and keep this food down, you can go home."

So I opened that applesauce, saltines, and tiny can of Sprite and ate them faster than I had ever eaten anything before. I had been a theatre minor, and in this moment, I was ready for my best performance because it was time to be done with this chapter of my life. I smiled and did a little dance. You see, my senior year in college as a theatre minor, I was forced to take a dance class. So I did a little jig and even a moonwalk. Of course, I was fighting through a dizzy, nauseating feeling and faking it the best I could, and I'm sure she knew it. But she smiled and lovingly said, "Tom, you did it. I want you to go home and rest."

I know she said more, but that's all I heard because I interrupted her words with a hug. A giant, loving, appreciative bear hug. "Thank you for being my angel today," I whispered, and she smiled with tears in her eyes to match mine. She walked me out to the waiting room doors, and I had done it. In fact, *we* had done it. All of you. All of us. We did that day together.

Ten

My Christmas Story

In some moments, we remember every smell, every breath; time stands still. Years later, we can describe the moment in detail to anyone who asks. In fact, this book has been full of such memories, and I've loved the chance to share my past with you. Too often in life, we forget the small stories that shape us in big ways, and we forget those relationships that matter deeply to us.

I wish this chapter could continue with such memories and stories. I wish I could describe every bit of what took place after those eventful days at the Mayo, but I can't. You see, I don't remember much of those days following my Gamma Knife procedure. I suppose medically, it's safe to say my brain was in trauma. This provides the right excuse for why I don't remember much. However, I have a different theory, and it's a fairly simple one. Bluntly, I think God was protecting me. Protecting me from remembering the sleepless nights, fear, and other shocks during those days, because the days that followed were some of the hardest in my life. With that said, I want you to understand as much as I *do* remember, and maybe the two of you will fill in some of what you remember along the way as well.

Walking out of that final Mayo room was so deeply freeing and yet so terrifying at the same time. I felt like I was floating as I walked, and I wasn't fully aware of what was going on around me. Of course, I do remember all of your faces in the waiting room, all the smiles when I entered, and also the visible relief that the procedure was finished. You had all come down in the early morning to be there for me when I came out of surgery. I think all of you must have thought I would instantly look different and were relieved when I looked rather normal. Yet in seeing you, I was fearful that the bandage around my head would scare you, but of course, you didn't blink an eye. I also loved your hugs and kindness and your grace when I don't think my words were coming out right in that moment. Finally, I appreciated that you didn't make a big deal out of it when they forced me to be wheeled me out of the hospital in that darn wheelchair. To be honest, it was embarrassing to be rolled out like that. I felt fragile and insecure as people looked at me. I could feel them staring at my bandaged head, creating stories in their minds about what had happened to me. As you can imagine, I was just focused on getting out of there, and having the two of you with me sure helped.

Once we were to our car, I somehow thought I was hungry. What is the deal with me feeling hungry when I'm really not? After I got my wisdom teeth out, I was hungry. Every single time I've had a fever, I've wanted McDonald's french fries. In this case, I wanted a sandwich from my new favorite local deli. Of course, I really wasn't hungry, yet I had convinced myself that "normal" people would eat, so I wanted to eat and appear to be normal for all of you. I wanted you to think I was perfectly fine after my procedure, and I figured if I ate with you, I could win you over. But once you were all back in the car (you ran in without me), that perfect sandwich got nibbled on a bit, but that was about it. My stomach sure was off during that drive home. With the trees whipping past us and my head spinning just as fast, it felt like I was on an amusement park ride I couldn't get off of. Plus my head hurt, so I tried to sleep—or at least faked sleeping to hide my true state of mind and feelings. I know I was too "off" feeling to use words, and I'm sure I was irrationally impatient, but you showed me grace.

Grace: a word and associated actions I've never been able to comprehend. In many ways, I don't think our minds can fully grasp grace. I know many people could define grace differently, but for me, I see it as receiving love when we don't necessarily deserve it. It's love when we least expect it, and it's love when we have done nothing to receive it. That's exactly what you gave me when you loved me as is and not as I should have been on my way home from the Mayo. You loved me even as I was feeling flawed, dizzy, and broken. You loved, and I'll never be able to show you my deep appreciation for that ride home. There I was, soaking up your grace, not knowing that you had more to give. Yet in the days to come, your grace and love would overflow.

On that drive home, I also texted all of the friends who chose to take this journey with me. I wanted them all to know I was safe and ok. I wanted them all to know how much I loved them and appreciated their words. In fact, when I turned my phone back on after the procedure, I was overwhelmed by all of their words of love and support. Often we don't know what to say in hard times, so we say nothing at all. But the reality is, during hard times people need to hear from us with even the smallest of words. Words of encouragement, shared memories, and words that allow us to process our thoughts and feelings, all help us to not feel alone in the process.

Those words carried me through that dizzy return drive, and by the time I got home, all I wanted to do was sleep. But I still had that darn headache that wouldn't go away. It was deeply painful and throbbed no matter what I did. I just couldn't get it to stop. I swear I could feel my heart beating in those four screw holes. I even tried forcing myself to lie down, yet the second I put my head back, the pressure of that soft pillow on my screw wounds was so deeply uncomfortable that I sat straight up and tried to keep my head from touching anything and everything. I've never been very good at sleeping upright, and it proved especially tough when trying to balance my head and sleep. I looked like a Bobblehead as I attempted to keep my head from touching anything close to those four wounds. It wasn't until two days later when my mom brought over her neck pillow that I was able to sleep a bit while upright.

The weeks following my procedure were full of sleepless nights, nights that contained far too many games on my iPhone and watching movies in the middle of the night. I wish I could do a better job of explaining how it felt, but in a nutshell, it felt like my mind was racing a million miles per hour—not with thoughts, but with a panicked feeling. That, combined with my uncomfortable, healing head, made it safe to say that sleeping wasn't my friend during that stage of my life. When you combine a lack of sleep, a healing brain stuck in a state of trauma, and an emotional response to all I was dealing with, it was not a season where I was at my best.

I wish I could say that the lack of sleep was the most challenging thing about the time after the procedure, but it wasn't. While December 23rd proved to be a great time to have my procedure due to the slower pace in my work schedule, that may have been selfish thinking because I think it proved to be quite painful for the two of you—especially with Christmas just two days later.

When I "woke" on Christmas Eve from my "nap" the night before, I had a hard time opening my eyes, especially the left one. It's safe to say you are slow at processing when your brain is in trauma, so my mind raced to understand what was wrong. First I wondered if I had gotten pink eye while I was in the hospital, and next I wondered if I was in the beginning stages of facial paralysis. When I reached up to feel my face with my hands, it just didn't feel right. Of course, standing quickly proved to be a challenge post-procedure, so I sat on the edge of the bed and focused my energy toward attempting to stand (and remain standing). I then slowly walked into the bathroom and tried to stay as quiet as possible since all of you were still sleeping. I flipped on that light and stood there, letting my eyes adjust before walking over to the mirror. When I had finally gotten myself to the mirror, I stood staring at a man I barely recognized.

The medical staff had mentioned that I would have some swelling, but this was far and above anything I had imagined. My eyes looked like Rocky Balboa after one of his fights. The screw entry points on my skin had swollen to what looked like large, black-and-blue half grapefruits. My forehead and eyes were so swollen that I could barely see, and the black-and-blue inflammation was like lava moving slowly down my face.

I began to panic when I figured out that I wasn't able to fully see. While I slowly walked into the kitchen, I felt the back of my head and realized it was just as swollen as the front. So I reached into the freezer and pulled out two ice packs to see if I could get the swelling down. Your mom, who had been sleeping in the basement, must have heard me, because when I shut the door to the freezer and turned, there she was.

I was surprised to see her standing there and having her see me in that state, and I thought that either my hearing was off, or I was just extremely focused on my own needs. The irony of that moment was that neither of us said a thing. In fact, there was a long pause as she stared at me and processed what she was seeing. It was probably a similar feeling to how I felt when I first saw myself in the mirror. I watched her quietly mouth "I'm sorry" as I walked silently back to the bedroom and put one ice pack on the back of my head and the other over the two wounds on the front. While I was icing, I tried to figure out why my front left side was so much worse than the right. Suddenly, I remembered that they had put more numbing solution on that side when I mentioned to the doctors that I still had feeling in that spot. Now I was lying there regretting those words to the doctor and, in fact, struggling with every bit of this process.

Maybe it was my lack of sleep. Maybe it was that I was still feeling the anxiety from the procedure itself. But seeing myself in that deformed, swollen state shook me. I kept that ice on and Advil in me all day long to try to get the swelling down so that I wouldn't scare the two of you. I made sure the swelling was at its very best before I would let the two of you see me later that day—Christmas Eve. It was one thing to hear about the procedure, but for the two of you to see the results of it on your daddy would have been overwhelming.

As you can imagine, Christmas Eve was lonely for me that year. Normally that would have been a day I would have loved finding ways to be close to the two of you. But that year, due to the physical and emotional impact of the procedure, I sadly admit that I tried to protect you by staying away that day. I guess I wasn't the only one feeling lonely that day. In all honesty, I don't know if such actions were fair to you. That was the thinking of a brain in trauma on an emotional day, and I guess at certain times in our lives, that's all we can do. We make decisions based on what we know, not what we don't, and then we deal with the consequences later.

Maybe that's why I'm writing this book to the two of you. Looking back, I don't know if I was rational enough to process the right information and emotions and to help you fully understand my journey. Of course, the writing of this book has provided healing to my own soul. But on that snowy Christmas Eve, I wasn't thinking as clearly as I can today.

I laid there icing, processing in an irrational way and found myself missing the small things I had previously loved sharing with the two of you. I missed laughing while watching *Elf*, and making soup, and, of course, the beautiful choir during the candlelight church service. I had tried to keep the day as normal as possible, so you and Mom went to church and to my parents' like previous years. Before you left, I dosed off. I woke up to a silent house with the exception of Christmas music coming from the kitchen radio. In fact, that's all I could hear: *Silent Night*, echoing throughout the house. I lay there in the darkness of the room, with my eyes swollen partially shut, and thought of the emotional irony of the moment. Just one day before I had been lying alone with my eyes closed, listening to a different kind of holiday music. Before I knew it, the tears streamed down my swollen face as I processed my journey over the previous forty-eight hours.

I think there are times in our lives that require every bit of our effort to create pure courage in order to get through them, and when we finally allow ourselves to come back to our "normal" state of being, our emotions overwhelm us. I wish I could say that this moment was the only time I relived the feelings of my Gamma Knife day, but I have felt them hundreds of times since. Some nights it's lying in bed with my eyes closed when suddenly, I'm back in that moment, and I wake to a racing heart. I usually don't put words to those thoughts and feelings that cause me to wake. The reality is, I'm trying to do the best I can to let you move on from that moment of time and not keep the family looking back at that moment. Rather, I want us focused on where we are going and on our hopeful future. But moments like those days at the Mayo stick with us. They become a part of our DNA and who we are. Now please know, they don't define us; they aren't who we are. Rather, they are a part of us and create a new lens to look through as we live life.

While I lay there, I tried to think of what I could do to calm myself. I realized I was in no state to do yoga, yet I didn't want to nap anymore. So I decided that a nice hot shower would calm me. I imagined how amazing that warm water flowing over my body would feel. But I was wrong. The second I felt the water hit my skin, it was like a thousand needles puncturing my skin all at once. No matter how cool I made the water temperature, the scalding pain continued. So I tried to wash my hair quickly (it had been three days), and yet again, the second the shampoo touched my scalp, it felt like my head was on fire. Every drop of water was like hot sauce being splashed into an open wound. I found myself standing at the far side of the tub, away from the water as I rushed to finish the cleansing process. What was supposed to be a relaxing shower ended up being one of the most painful experiences of my life.

By the time you arrived home from church, I had composed my emotions yet was still feeling extremely uncomfortable. I was nauseated, and every movement made me feel sick to my stomach. To add to that, I just hurt. But it wasn't just my head that hurt: even my body was sore, and the shower had elevated that feeling. I guess that Gamma Knife couch wasn't good for the bod, although it's safe to say that my uptight muscles probably didn't help. I guess sore was the new normal for the situation. "One day at a time" is all I kept telling myself. In fact, I'm not sure what else I *could* have told myself. I could be a victim to my circumstances, or I could rise above all that I was feeling. I chose to rise above it, although at any given second, that was an internal battle. Sometimes my will won, and sometimes the pain won.

Our Christmas Eve ended with me slowly making my way to the living room to share in our annual "one gift" evening for the two of you. Now, I'm sure you were surprised to open your boxes to find pajamas, once again, but just like other traditions, you smiled big and thanked us for the gift. You then went to your rooms to change and try on your new pajamas, and with that, I was back to the bedroom to attempt to sleep as you did the same. While traditionally you often struggled with sleeping on Christmas Eve, I think you may have had better luck than I that night.

I awoke on Christmas morning after a limited sleep the night before. When I attempted to open up my eyes as I stretched, I couldn't do so. My partially swollen eyes were now completely swollen shut to the point where I couldn't see out of them at all. I experienced such an instant panic that it felt like running out of air while swimming. I reached up to see if I could spread the swollen skin apart so I could see, but it was an impossible task. With a racing, fearful heart, I lay there quietly crying for a bit, but even my tears made my skin burn. So I calmed myself by taking long, deep yoga breaths before reaching over to my side table and feeling around to find the sunglasses I had worn the day before to hide my swollenness. I squeezed them over my inflamed head and called each of you in one at a time.

I wanted to share with you my new state of being and to do so proactively so that seeing me wouldn't scare you. So I called you each into my darkened room, one person at a time. I began by calmly explaining that I couldn't open up my eyes and that when I turned on the lights, you would see your dad's face looking even more swollen and more black and blue than the day before. I also talked to you about how it might feel overwhelming to see, especially in your daddy. Finally, I prepared you that I was going to keep my sunglasses on for the day to hide myself a bit, but I was going to still be with you for as much of Christmas day as

I could handle. I vividly remember each of your responses that showed such powerful, overwhelming care and love. Today as I write these words, the tears stream down my face as I relive that deep, loved feeling you created for me. You both held me and whispered that I was ok like I had done for you years earlier when you were young. There I was, bringing you into my room to try to take care of you, and instead I was given a gift of a twelve and fourteen year old reversing the conversation and pouring their love into their daddy.

Once I had individually finished the conversation with each of you, you both came in the room together and cuddled in close and let me hold you. In that brief moment, I felt like a healed man again. In that moment, I wasn't black and blue, my skin wasn't burning, and I could see your beauty once again. In that moment, I got to be Daddy again. While I couldn't see you, I could feel your breathing aligned with mine, and I could feel your warm bodies perfectly wrapped in my 6'4" frame. Right there in that moment was my Christmas gift. A gift that I will never forget and will always be able to describe in detail because of its impact. Thank you for that gift and for your love to a wounded daddy.

Eleven

My New Four-Burner Stovetop

I love to cook. Quite simply, it's become my favorite new hobby as I love to learn more about how to create the perfect dish. I find cooking to be an introvert's dream come true in the quiet of the creativity-filled kitchen. To date, my favorite meal contains a perfect combination of sweet and spicy. Dishes that include honey, mint, and basil plus some hot red peppers are like a rainbow in my stomach. Neither part of the dish overwhelms the other, and that's where the perfect balance takes place. My favorite dish to cook is a sweet and spicy chili that bypasses traditional chili powder and high-sodium additives. Instead, I use dark beer and dark chocolate to balance jalapeños, hot red peppers, and Tabasco, plus fresh herbs and veggies.

Along the way, I've also learned that the perfect dish will have a balanced amount of acid in it as well. Too much and the dish could be ruined, not enough and you'd know something is off. The challenge for me is that I believe I never have, and never will, master the perfect dish. I think a meal can always be better and perfected even more, so I remain on an endless search for the perfect balance.

As I entered into January and February following my procedure, I was feeling anything but balanced and whole. My life felt as unbalanced as I have ever experienced, and the result was a personality that often felt far more spicy than sweet. In fact, I think it's safe to say there were times that I was downright salty. I don't think any of us would look back on this season and say, "Dad was sure at his best."

While I was slowly feeling less sore and a bit better, I was also feeling deeply off, and I was a walking flytrap for disease. The second I was around anyone with a cold or flu, I would get it. If someone sneezed around me, it seemed like mere minutes before I would feel the cold permeate my system. I think it's safe to guess that my immune system was busy doing other things during this season, because I was sick a lot. I would also guess that the stress I was under wasn't helping me stay healthy either. I literally spent more time in the doctor's office in those few months following my procedure than I had in my entire lifetime.

Now, you can imagine how hard it was to attempt to heal from such a major procedure. However, one gift in the healing process was working for an organization that let me come back to work slowly and having a perfect boss (Connie) who continued to check in on me through the entire process. It's amazing to me how much loyalty that season created for me with my workplace, Gallup. The leaders and my work family who reached out to me almost daily, plus coworkers like Jim and Mark who were going through their own "health stuff," mattered deeply to me. In addition, my coworker Tom had been the one to send me the new research articles about brain tumors, which began my journey to Mayo and to my Gamma Knife choice.

If more organizations could simply embrace their employees during times of struggle and treat them with even half of the same respect I was shown, they would create an army of employees that would go above and beyond for that organization. When that type of engagement takes place, employees simply can't imagine a world without the company that has impacted them so. Gallup has become one such an organization for me, and it feels like family.

My doctor's office also created the same type of deep personal engagement. Now, I want to be clear. I'm not describing satisfaction, which I think people often confuse with engagement. Engagement is far and beyond simple satisfaction. When we are engaged, we make bold emotional statements about the customer experience, and it feels personal, while an experience that leaves us satisfied simply met our basic needs. In my case, while I loved my doctor's office, I don't think it was the office staff or waiting room chairs that created the deep level of engagement I felt. Rather, it was my family doctor.

Since I was sick so often after the procedure, I was seeing him weekly, but he wasn't just a prescribing doctor. Rather, he took on the role of cheerleader, counselor, and friend. He took the time to be fully present and observe my nonverbal communication, even how I was sitting in the chair. He described that, in one stage, I would come in, take a seat, sit straight up, and nervously play with my fingernails. (He finally knew I was better when he saw me slouching and smiling again while responding with sarcasm.) My doctor kindly held up a "mirror" to tell me what he was seeing and feeling. Never did I feel rushed or uncared for.

When we are given such deep levels of customer service we can't stop talking about it, customers like me become the best salesmen, marketers, and public relation champions for that organization. In fact, I think I have recruited more friends to that clinic, and specifically to my family doctor, than I could begin to count. But that's what we do when we are treated as we should be. I often think about my own clients and whether or not I'm creating the kind of engaging relationship Dr. Peterson and Gallup created for me, because I can't imagine a world without either one.

I wish I could say that my high level of engagement got me through this season of life, but that's just not reality. One of the things I was slowly learning is that I wasn't able to do some of the things I used to. For example, I used to pride myself on my ability to multitask, and my friends always looked at my balanced schedule and asked how I did it. For me, it wasn't hard. I've always loved having multiple things going on in my life all at once. I loved volunteering with Sigma Chi, coaching tennis, attending grad school, and still being present with my family and friends. I'm sure I gave up something along the way, but somehow that juggling allowed me to hone my focus. But that was the old me, and this was the new me. Suddenly, balls I used to love to juggle were falling all around me, and I just couldn't get ahead.

About the same time I went through my procedure, my good friend Tony had a major brain injury. He was off by himself in the woods of northern Wisconsin riding a four-wheeler, and he hit a deer, causing him to fly over the handlebars. The brain trauma he suffered seemed similar to what I was dealing with while recovering from both Gamma Knife and my third major concussion. I think I often forgot the fact that I wasn't just dealing with the procedure but was also still in the lengthy recovery from my concussion that started this whole journey.

As sat discussing our new realities with Tony, we found comforting similarities. We no longer were as social, could no longer handle the noise of a busy coffee shop, and were both instantly irritated by new sounds that we had never noticed before. Plus, we would both be "shut down" by our brain at times, and we had to learn to not fight through it but to simply accept our new reality. He shared with me his doctor's new description of his life, and upon hearing the analogy, I found those words to be the perfect descriptor for my new state of being.

He compared personalities like ours to the fancy, five-burner stovetops. We could have all five burners in use and not miss a beat. In fact, it felt natural to us to juggle that many things at once, and we couldn't figure out how others couldn't do the same. However, following my procedure and his head trauma, we no longer had that fancy middle burner. It was simply gone. While it was still a beautiful stove capable of amazing things, it could no longer handle five things all at once. It was up to us to accept our four burners and quit fighting to get more on the stovetop.

In those four to six months that followed my procedure, I had to learn how to say no and adjust to my new reality. I slowly learned that I could no longer be all things to all people. As easy as that may sound, it was actually a painful, awkward lesson for me to learn, and it's one I still struggle to accept to this day. I daily find myself trying to be the "old me," taking on more then my four burners can handle. On my work team and in my life, I had a pattern of over-scheduling meetings and then canceling right beforehand when I felt my brain shutting down. I felt like I was an awkward middle school boy who had gone through a growth spurt and no longer remembered how to run. I knew that my four-burner stovetop felt different—not bad, not worse, but different—and I was fighting the awkwardness of the run the entire time.

One of my challenges was that people couldn't see what I was dealing with since it wasn't an external ailment. While I was thankful I didn't have any exterior physical damage at that stage, I sure still felt off on the inside. I felt different, and my brain wasn't working the same, yet I looked normal (at least, as normal as I ever look). The first time I went to the office, some well-meaning coworkers boldly and lovingly stated, "Wow, you don't look bad at all. We thought you would look horrible, but you look normal." So I learned to use words to describe my state of mind and my state of wellbeing, something I was simply horrible at doing at the time, but the more I did so, the more those loving coworkers could understand the new me. My challenge was that, somehow, it felt like I was being negative. I wasn't used to complaining, and I tended to avoid those who did. But I had to learn that others around me couldn't read my mind, and since they couldn't see what I was feeling or reacting to, they needed my words to fully understand.

"What do you need?" has become one of my favorite questions to ask of others because of this process. A "need" question elicits a reaction that is the combo of the emotional and physical and is a true gut reaction. Upon asking that question, I've heard responses ranging from "a hug," to "a listening ear," to "help creating action." It's a question that gets at the core of what a person is really asking for. In fact, it's actually a fair question to repeat if you are looking for more than a surface response. It was also a question I needed to ask myself a lot and one I valued others asking of me as well. I think what I was figuring out during this early season is that I wasn't very good at naming my own needs and naming my true physical state. Somehow I had always been able to accomplish all that I wanted and needed on my own, and not being able to do so felt foreign.

Now you may find it odd that a professional speaker was struggling to find the right words to use. Previously, I talked about how much I love words and how they are so fascinating to me. But these words were different and far more personal. I wasn't up in front, authentically speaking and finding the perfect words for a perfect story to make a point. In this case, the words described struggles and shifts that I was dealing with emotionally for the first time. I had to also deal with those I loved and cared for hearing for the first time about my new four-burner stove. They heard me say no to things I had done in the past. Admitting my new world made me vulnerable and proved to be one of the most challenging aspects of this process. When you grow up being told you can do anything you want to do, you believe it and act on it. So not being able to do what I wanted was embarrassing; and to admit it verbally felt even worse and more painful.

My slowly shifting Superman mindset was also changing how I could perform my role at work. Shortly after my procedure, I had a trip scheduled to Allentown, PA, where I was going to speak to educators at one of my favorite colleges in the United States: Muhlenberg College. After the two days of teaching, I was also going to keynote at a leadership event for the school. The trip was going to take four days of my time, effort, and brainpower. It was so soon after my procedure that I should have just said no, but I didn't. Instead, I flew out and taught the first full day, which took everything out of me.

Post-session, I stopped by a local place to get some sushi for dinner on the way home. That night I became so violently sick I had to cancel my second day of teaching. In fact, I was so sick that I wasn't able to leave my bed and was stuck in a foreign city, painfully alone. I didn't want to admit what had just taken place, so I blamed the sushi and made jokes with the school leaders about not eating the sushi in the area, but I knew the reality: my immune system wasn't right, and it was too soon for me to be traveling, but I was too embarrassed to say so. While I had enough energy to keynote for the final day's leadership event, after that trip I canceled my next three speaking events. I was being forced to allow myself to still heal while adjusting to my new stove.

Those next three weeks at home were healthy for me as I found myself relaxing a bit more and learning to take care of myself. I even slept all the way through the night for a few nights! My doctor began seeing me less often, and my new normal was becoming a bit more comfortable. But every single day when I left the house go to work, run errands, and just get out, I knew that, though I looked the same and drove the same car, I was different. My brain just wasn't as fast as it had been, and my headaches remained. I was the same person, but I didn't feel like the same person. During that stage of life, I felt like I was living an out-of-body experience. I tried to be a good dad, good family member, and good friend, but I didn't feel great at any one thing. Oh, how I desired to feel great at something again! I think we all want that. We all want to shine. We all want to thrive. When life knocks us down, it can be scary and painful to get up. I knew it was just a season, but I wanted it to be done.

Twelve

New Books, New Values

I love reading and am one of those readers that always has multiple books going all at once. My side table can often look like a game of Jenga as I attempt to stack my books in a way that won't have them tumble down in the night. Every night I look at my stack, and pick one book carefully out of the pile without disrupting it. Typically my chosen book depends on my mood and having book choices is important to me. During this in-between stage of life, I was stuck between recovery mode and waiting mode and my books reflected that. I again wasn't sure if my procedure had worked and nor was I sure of the full complications of my procedure either. In addition, I didn't know how to respond to people when they asked how I was feeling and was in a messy, purgatory state of mind.

I found myself reading every and any book focused on Positive Psychology, well-being, happiness, hope and creativity. I soaked up authors views on my mindset, healing and growth and began to shift how I was viewing my future.

Previously, my past life has always felt like a book series that comes together to form one long story full of different characters and plots. Like any good writer, the writing of my life books has matured over time as I became more comfortable letting my words flow freely. Sometimes those words feel challenging and forced, while other times they feel deeply connected to my soul. Along the way, each book fleshes out new characters that entered my life, and each person, process, job, change, etc. has changed my writing and the outcome of each book.

My life has been a process of developing my own character and understanding how each chapter has come together in these books to form the story of Tom Matson. Sometimes I've written a book from the perspective of a hero, while other times I've found myself writing from a victim lens. I've also found that there are many chapters within these books that were peaks for my friends while for me, they didn't have the same impact. My books were often filled with small chapters that many wouldn't have valued. Yet, looking back, they were the biggest seasons of my life in terms of learning and change. For many of my friends, graduating from college was one of the greatest chapters in their life. While that is indeed an amazing accomplishment, for me, it was anticlimactic as I simply walked away from my friends and the life I had come to know to begin a new chapter of adulthood and working. I think for many of us, leaving college forced us to attempt to understand who we are in this world while also trying to understand what the world wants from us. Graduating was the beginning of a new book, and I'm not sure I was ready for the old one to end. New books can equate to growth if we let them, but I wasn't always open to such thinking.

In my 20s, you would have observed me writing my life book as an attempt to make bold, absolute statements that showed others how smart I was and what an amazing mind I had. Maybe such a representation was due to my own insecurity, but I deeply desired to have people see me as smart, someone who had it all together. So I put together a perfectly organized book full of "I" statements and impressive details about myself. Sadly, a life book written through such a lens puts people on the defense far more than it creates learning and conversation. In fact, I often found myself talking *at* people more than talking *with* people. The result was that our conversation turned into a debate more than a true chance to learn from each other, yet I often missed the social cues that there was any discomfort for others in such moments.

Months out from my procedure, I was feeling far removed from this bold former self I had written about in my 20s life book. To this day, I still deeply value a strong statement that leads to conversation, but based on all that I was reading and learning, that mindset is very different than making bold statements simply to look smart and create debate. I often wondered if I could throw away that former book and just allow people to read this new book that was being written. But, that's not how life works. So there are many people out there who see me as very different from the person I am today. Some may miss that previous Tom and some would love the new me if they truly got to know me today. But not everyone wants to take the time to remove me from the box they had put me in previously. Sadly, they were missing out on the "new me"; I truly felt different as I interacted with people during this new chapter. This "new me" was far more interested in hearing about others and their stories. I valued the perfect question more than the perfect statement, and I valued the chance to really hear someone out and understand their values and lens through which they viewed the world.

Not only was I interested in others' values but I found myself thinking about my own world differently. My lens was changing and so was my new life book: it felt far more like long-term change than just a short-term, emotional change. The life I desired was a very different life than the one I had previously valued. In fact, values were on my mind daily, and such thoughts began sneaking into every conversation I would watch some friends embrace challenging life questions about why they believe what they do while others struggled to wrap their minds around what I was asking and why. I found that some would tell me what they thought I wanted to hear or what they were supposed to value, while others were authentic in questioning what their values truly were.

For the first time in my life, I was forcing myself to look into a mirror and ask myself what values guided me and whether or not I was truly living by what I professed. For years, I had found myself going through the motions of saying the "right things," knowing how to act in any situation. In fact, if I would have walked down a street full of coffee shops and stopped into each one filled with different groups of people from my life, I could have instantly fit in and talked their talk. Yet if they were all together in a room, they would have been confused by my inconsistent behaviors and words. That life no longer felt authentic to me, so I was done being a chameleon lens in life. I wanted to live authentically and truly be me. I wanted to walk into those coffee shops and interact with every group consistently. That meant authentically living out this new me and new life book.

So I began to journal about my true core values, and not just the ones the world professed as valuable. The more I reflected, the more my life and values became clearer, and it's no surprise that I found myself liking who I was more than ever before. I was far less interested in how others in the world responded to me and celebrated me. Instead, I valued this new life book as one that was full of writing about the authentic me, written from the perspective of someone who was comfortable in his own skin for the first time.

For years, while the world was celebrating my roles as a speaker, coach, consultant, and more, I was falling short of fully knowing who I was. In my coaching of leaders and others, I've learned that far too many of us struggle to truly know our values and ourselves. But that life lens is a lonely perspective that keeps too many people at arm's length. Maybe we fear that others may learn that we aren't perfect and see the flawed, normal versions of us. In addition, we lose sight of the blessings of our lives when such thinking paralyzes us.

The people around us in life deserve to see all of us. They deserve to know the good and celebrate the uniqueness of our life books that have been previously written. Why aren't we asking others about such things as well? I deeply believe that if all of us took the time to ask such questions of each other, the world would look different. We all need to know where we are at our best, and we all need to help others recognize the same about themselves.

So as your dad, Morgan and Tyler, I want to do my very best to help you know who you are in this world. For the early years of your lives, I was writing your life books for you, but now you are at ages where you are writing your own. I often wonder what it's like to grow up in this new world of technology. How does it shape how you think, feel, and act? I wonder how technology changes how you write your life books and how it impacts your values and lens on this world. I also wonder what that pressure feels like to have all the newest phones and technology.

I want you both to know, I see how technology is so important to your friends and to those around you. I deeply wish I could give you both amazing phones like so many of your friends have, but our values keep me from doing so. It's not that I don't want you to be able to communicate (which is why you both have phones), but we need to make values-based decisions and live within a budget that is aligned with our family values. Sadly, too many of our friends don't know what it's like to live within their means and instead live with tremendous debt in a world of overspending. Living within our financial values lead us to make such decisions that may not make sense to those around us. So because of that, I don't have the newest clothes, and I don't have the newest car, and I buy things that will last for a long time, even if they aren't the most trendy.

But stewardship wins, and such values have allowed us to afford to send you to the school that we do. That's what values do. They guide us in how we make decisions and in how we interact with others. They are the core of who we are and what makes us tick. So as your dad, after what I have gone through, I not only want you to understand my values, but I want to help you write your life books through your own values lens too. In fact, knowing that you are writing your own life books is why I ask so many questions, like how you sort your decision-making and friendships. I'm asking to help you know yourselves! So please know how I see you. Please know how I celebrate your unique gifts.

Tyler, my wonderful son, I deeply value how you love to learn and grow. I also love that you value shared experiences with me. From skiing in the mountains of Colorado, to cuddling up watching a movie, to simply fixing something together. You allow yourself to be fully present, and when you do, we are blessed by pure, authentic, loving moments. Even the small moments when we go outside to throw a football or baseball are highlights of my life I reflect on daily. They fill my soul because I know in those moments, if I simply allow myself to be quiet, your words will begin to fill the air.

I soak up that gift of hearing you process, and I love to hear you tell me about what you saw that day. I know you share those thoughts not only to allow me to see what you see but also because you value getting my reflections on what you are feeling as well. When your thoughts and feelings are finally at the point of flowing into words, it means you have spent a considerable amount of time thinking about them before I had the honor to hear them. But, for me, it's in such moments that I can help you process and celebrate who you are. It's in those moments that I'm allowed to hold up a mirror so you can understand your values and what guides you. I love all those parts of you plus millions more (including your amazing sense of humor).

Morgan, my beautiful daughter, I love your smile and authentic joy. To this day, I remember your first baby giggle that made me feel so deeply connected to you, and I have loved each heartwarming giggle since. You've given me the gift of hundreds of equally impactful moments that we have shared together. We've spent time walking around DC, enjoying torchlight Christmas Eves in Colorado, and hitting on the tennis court for thousands of hours, talking about who you seek to be as a tennis player.

Who do you seek to be? That's something we talk about a lot. In fact, when we talk about it on the tennis court, I'm simply using the experience to talk about who you are in life. At the core of who you are, I see you wanting to impact others and make a difference in their lives—and you're gifted at both. I love that you love to observe people rather than be the center of attention, yet at your very best moments, you are surrounded by kids and people of all ages, loving them as is and helping them grow. I hope I give that gift right back to you. I hope I can impact you like you do others. I'm so deeply impressed by you, your heart and your values.

While I love chances to hold up a mirror for the two of you, allowing you to know yourselves more, I value the same in my own life. That's why this was such an important state of my life as this new life book was being written. With every new book, it felt like a giant mirror was being held up in front of me daily, and it was changing who I was and how I wanted to impact this world (and even the two of you). Here I was with a "broken brain," loving every new lens and new value I was thinking about and acting on daily. This amazing brain tumor was changing me in ways that I never knew possible. Ironically, while I loved this new me, I'm not sure everyone else felt the same. You see, I'm not sure the world around us always wants us to change. Our changes force them to shift some things in their own lives, plus check their assumptions at the door. Though we may love our shifts and growth, the discomfort it brings others may just be too much for them.

The result of my changes during this book of life led to some friendships lost - and others gained. I pulled back from some "friends" that I had known for years, while drew closer to others who matched my growth mentality. It also meant that I stopped doing some things I had previously invested in as I started new well-being traditions and new healthy habits. True friends see that and stick with us through such changes, while others won't. But we need to be comfortable enough with ourselves to know that not everyone will embrace our changes, and that's ok. So I want the two of you to be you, and not the person your friends and world think you should be. Trust me, your true friends will still be there while the ones that maybe shouldn't have been there to begin with will fade away.

My value shifts began as small changes and grew over time, and my confidence in trusting my heart also increased. I found myself examining how and where I spent my time in order to align with my values. I see life as short and precious, and thus, our time in life should connect to our values. This new lens on life created the need for me to change, so suddenly, the three different nonprofit boards I was serving on didn't feel as valuable as they once had. But as I said earlier, while I was soaking up the new and growing me, I think it felt personal to those on the boards when I put in my resignation. It wasn't that the board and mission of the organizations lacked value; rather, it was the time they took away from things I valued more. I was drawing bold lines in the sand about time well spent and time well valued. If I had to choose between serving on a board for an amazing nonprofit or watching a movie cuddled up with the two of you, going on a long walk, and having a cup of coffee with a dear friend, it was an easy choice. To live a value like "life is short" means our time commitments match up with such guiding principles. No more lip service, just words and actions coming together.

I also began examining how the people in my life were impacting me. For most of my life, I took great pride in counseling people and serving as a mentor to far too many. If I was truly honest with myself, I think I was mentoring because it looked good to others and made me feel important. The result of such needy thinking was that I often met with people who were either lost or needed far too much emotional guidance. While I have no problem helping guide people in life, the challenge for me came with people who were stuck in negative or dysfunctional patterns. I would leave such meetings emotionally dry, carrying their negative energy with me into other areas of my life. But with my growing values, I couldn't authentically keep contagious, negative people in my life. Life was a gift, and I wanted to put myself near others who embraced a similar mindset.

I boldly and quickly decided to change with whom to spend my time. I quit hanging out with negative people, and instead tightened my circle of friends and surrounded myself with people who were positive, loving, and trying to be healthy. I wanted to be around people who didn't demand emotional attention I was unable to provide, without giving anything in return. The reality is, we can handle one, maybe two, people who steal our emotional mojo. I didn't need to be needed by many. Instead, I wanted to connect with the right friends that I also needed in return. I needed true friendships and true authentic conversations. The kinds of conversations that fill our souls and we can't wait to have again. Now those are friends who make life worth living. So I guarded my time and made bold relational changes. Ironically, I've never felt happier and more alive. I guess if you put negativity into your mind and soul, life looks and feels negative. In turn, if you put positive people around you, your lens on life will be impacted as well.

Of course, it was far easier to shift the people who are in my life outside of work than those who are inside. Getting along with the people we work with can feel like forced relationships, and this can either be a gift, or it can be emotionally painful for us. So I found myself sorting at work as well, spending more time with those who gave me life. Learning to make such changes and learning from others who love what they do created an incredible medicine for my soul. Suddenly, my relationships at work were as valuable and healthy as those outside of work. Small choices with our time and energy lead to large rewards.

I also was beginning to understand what it truly meant to own my choices, words, and actions. I valued an authentic apology and conversations about where I had fallen short. As your dad, I know the two of you have sure felt that as I tried to be the best dad possible but, in my humanness, fell short. I'm amazed at how many people fail to own their mistakes. For them, it's always someone else's fault, and they seem to be stuck looking at life through a victim mindset.

A victim mindset is one that guides far too many into thinking that everyone else is broken and everyone else is messing up. It simply can't be *them* making the mistake; rather, it's everyone else's fault. I love to ask them, "And what part of that do you own?"

They often will stare at me blankly and respond with a flippant, "I guess I cared *too* much," which again lacks ownership. No matter how many questions I asked them about their ownership and learning, they couldn't take it upon themselves to have any personal takeaways, so sadly, their patterns in life continue to this day. You see, owning our mistakes and learning from them is a part of truly living an authentic, values-based life. Life is too short not to. Plus I value the learning and growth. If I'm not open to true feedback and learning, I'm missing the gift of growth. So I think post-tumor Tom has said "I'm sorry" more than I had in the previous forty-plus years of my life. By so doing, I've grown in my understanding of myself more than ever before. What a gift.

I found myself rejoicing in my shifts and feeling more comfortable with myself than ever before. Don't you see the irony of that? The result of this darn tumor, which created so much fear and anxiety, was a world that I was reaping the benefits of daily. Up until this tumor was diagnosed, I had spent the majority of my life chasing the next thing. The next resume builder, the next impressive role, and the next way the world would value my contributions. Yet I was missing truly living every day and fully being present in life and it took a tumor to slow me down to learn such things.

Thirteen

The Sands of Time

"Like sands through the hourglass, so are the days of our lives."
Every single day upon returning to my dorm room from class, I
would hear those very powerful words. My roommate Rob had been
a high school wrestler, and he was a walking, talking example of
a traditional wrestler. But Rob had one thing that made him a bit
different from other wrestlers, and it all began with that quote. Not
only did Rob live by that motto daily, but Rob also lived for the
foundation of that motto. Rob had an addiction to the soap opera
Days of our Lives. Not only did he never miss it, he loved to hear
that quote daily at the beginning of the show.

First semester, he strategically scheduled his classes around his soap
opera addiction. Now, I guess there are worse addictions for your
college roommate to have, but at first it was rather annoying. I was

in my triple room with Rob and Andy, and we only had one TV, so we were forced to join into Rob's addiction. Early in the semester, the second the show started, Andy would get up and walk out, but over time he started to remain in the room. At first he acted like he wasn't paying attention to it and instead would shine his pleather Velcro shoes. But in time, that shoeshine brush was placed off to the side and his eyes became glued to that magical 10-inch TV screen.

I had a similar initial reaction and would fake studying, but in time I, too, was hooked. After a few months, the three of us would get our lunches to go and meet right at noon to experience the life-changing stories together. Second semester, it wasn't just Rob arranging his schedule to make sure he didn't miss the soap: it was all three of us. Actually, that's how I ended up taking geology, where I got the first D of my life (I'm not good at memorizing the names of rocks). The science course I truly wanted to take (astronomy) would have conflicted with our soap, so I figured rocks couldn't be too much different from stars.

Throughout that first year, we lived through the characters on the show and even found ourselves talking about them at night while we were going to bed. Sadly, it got to the point that we were talking about them like we knew them, like they were real people. (That may have been when it was time to admit our problem). But that show did what nothing else had been able to do: it brought together this unlikely trio of roommates and forged a friendship around, of all things, a soap opera. While we loved the experience of the show, we faced a daily challenge when every episode ended with a cliffhanger, thus leaving us to wonder what would happen next. Ironically, the daily cliffhanger wasn't the most challenging part. Rather, it was the weekends when we had to wait almost three days to know what was going to happen next. Oh, how I hated waiting!

I've never been at my best when waiting is involved. Even at the wise age of 19, I was still impatient when waiting for news and cliffhangers. I hated amusement parks for that reason. The lines were just too painful to me; when I was ready to ride, I was ready to ride! Waiting in line for an hour to get to the front just didn't seem worth it. Even applying to colleges was painful, and I've struggled with impatiently waiting on other life news as well. I want to know yesterday, and today is too late. Anything longer than that feels unbearable.

Maybe it was control issue. Maybe it was that I didn't like wondering how the end result would make me feel. Maybe I was just impatient. But throughout my lifetime, I have always believed my hard work and actions could control my future, and I felt like I deserved to know that future now. I had learned that whatever I set my mind to, I could accomplish. But applying to colleges, jobs, or even waiting for new episodes of a soap opera took the control out of my hands and into the hands of another.

One year removed from my procedure, I was still dealing with my control issues, even though this process had reminded me over and over that I wasn't in control. In the eyes of most, this episode in my life was in my past. I am daily asked, "Aren't you glad to have that behind you?"

The reality was, I only had one thing behind me: the procedure. But that's what most people were focused on, and that's what most people remembered. Maybe I created that thinking by talking about the procedure alone and not the process that took place afterward.

It was easy to do at the time because of how scary the actual surgery felt to me. It's easy to focus on specific moments and not the *outcomes* of those moments. I'm afraid that, though I had talked a lot about Gamma Knife early on, I was now failing to allow people to understand all that would follow.

If I had chosen cranial surgery over Gamma Knife, it would have been an event with more "instant" results. I would have known shortly after the procedure whether they had been able to fully remove the tumor or not. Of course, the healing would have still been a challenge with the unknowns about the future implications of the procedure. However, Gamma Knife simply started the process, and it created a long road ahead full of unknowns—a challenge for someone who struggles with control. It can takes years to feel the effects of the Gamma Knife procedure as the tumor and its surrounding area scar. It's a slow, impatience-filled process that led me to feel powerless at many steps along the way. I had no way of knowing what was next and no way of knowing if it had worked or not.

There were steps along the way to check in and see some early results. At the six-month point, I had an MRI to simply see the initial results of the procedure. It was an odd feeling to be back down at Mayo getting an MRI, and I found myself reliving all those memories and emotions. In many ways, it felt like I was going through the entire process all over again. But in this case, the results weren't going to show us anything actionable. They weren't going to show us if the procedure had worked; rather, they felt like a college midterm to simply check in on my short-term progress.

My early results showed that the procedure had indeed changed the tumor, but the news itself confused me. I thought we were looking for the mass to shrink in size, but when I got my results back, it actually showed that there had been growth. My doctor reminded me that my brain was still in trauma, and, like a sprained ankle or other injury, it was still swollen from the effects of the procedure. Based on that, I liked to joke that my tumor was still angry and acting out, so of course it looked different at the six-month point.

But like sands through the hourglass, time went on, and I was counting down the days till my one-year checkup and like sands through the hourglass, time went on, as I counted down the days till my one-year checkup. The thoughts that daily ran through my mind felt far more in control of me than I did over them. While I found myself establishing new values for how I was living life, I struggled with my self-talk as I approached that December date.

Isn't that interesting how that works? Everything around me should have felt good. I wasn't dealing with much in terms of complications. Though there had been small changes, I simply assumed they would go away in time. Occasionally, a ringing sound surfaced in my ear, and sometimes my face felt numb, but they never stuck. So I had a million reasons to feel positive, safe, and good, yet I still struggled with the unknowns and how I would respond to the news. I just wanted to know what that one-year appointment would tell me, and as that date approached, I could feel the questions flowing through my mind constantly.

What if the Gamma Knife hadn't truly worked? What would happen in December if they found the tumor had continued to grow? I was told early in the process that I would have one shot for the Gamma Knife to work, and if it didn't, they couldn't do it again. They would have no other choice but to perform cranial surgery to remove it. But it wouldn't be like the previous procedure because the tumor and the area around it would have changed. The doctors would be performing surgery to the best of their abilities in an area now damaged and scarred by radiation. So the complications of such a procedure were far greater than before. The chances of full hearing loss, facial drop, balance issues, etc. were also far higher than before.

Isn't it interesting how self-talk can control us and our thoughts? I remember walking into the bathroom and staring at myself in the mirror, wondering what facial drop would look like. I pulled down the skin around my eye and stared at myself as I tried to prepare myself for the possibilities and think of how I would find comfort in my new look and other changes. In fact, such thoughts were even on my mind when I glanced in my rearview while driving—more and more every time I felt my face tingle.

I was still trying to be present in life, but while I was there physically, my mind was focused on other thoughts. Our minds are both an incredible part of our human body and a challenge to control at the same time. Sometimes I had the ability to calm my inner voice, and other times my self-talk won. That inner voice also started to shift how I was doing life in small ways, even if I didn't realize it at the time. I began to create tiny shifts in my role at work that would allow me to be behind the scenes if I had to have cranial surgery. I was doing shorter strategy sessions and more phone executive coaching in case I could no longer be in front of clients and audiences. Our self-talk can create change even when we don't know that's exactly what's taking place.

As I approached my appointment, I found myself going back into my mind far more than I wanted. I was trying my best to remain true to my new values and new lens, but it felt like a daily internal debate. I overanalyzed and created results of the appointment in my mind, before it had even took place. By the time the appointment occurred, my emotions were in overdrive, and my impatience with the process was at an all-time high. I simply wanted my appointment over with, and I wanted to know the results.

My appointment was again close to the holidays, which were creating more time for phone calls and coffee with friends. Many of us reach out intentionally to more friends and loved ones during that time of year. Some were people I hadn't talked with in close to a year, while others were friends who had taken this entire journey with me. If you want to know who your true friends are, go through something major like this. The true friends are right there, even when it's tiring for them. Others who had claimed to be friends simply weren't living out my new view of true, authentic friendships.

One of the things I have learned in this process is how not to interact with people during tragedy and life struggles. I've learned what true friendship means and what feels inauthentic as well. I still remember a card one of my friends received upon the death of his child. It said something like, *so sorry for your loss. There is a flower in heaven today because of your child.* I know I'm not quoting the card quite right, and I'm sure someone may be offended by my response. Maybe someone spent a long time writing that card, but every time I read it, I threw up in my mouth a bit and was offended by how fake it felt to me. My friend didn't want a sappy card; he wanted authentically caring people to ask him how he was. He wanted people who would come back years later and ask more about him and his life, not letting him forget his amazing son.

In this process, I wanted that same type of authenticity. I didn't want to have to deal with people telling me they were glad it was behind me. I wanted people who were willing to be real and ask real questions. I wanted friends like my mentor Greg, who wasn't satisfied with the generic response when he asked me how my health was and I responded with, "Oh, it's ok. Thanks so much for asking." But such a response is what 99% of the world is looking for. I was often reminded during this process that people asked about me because they were supposed to, but I'm also quite sure they didn't want any greater response than the generic one I had mastered. But Greg did, and he lovingly pushed and asked me how I was really doing and what getting the results had felt like and how it had impacted my daily life. Friends like Greg are friends we need in such a process. They want to ask questions not because they are supposed to but because they want to authentically hear our response and stick by us no matter what.

Because of how I was reacting to the generic people in my life, on the date of my recheck, I had just told a few people about the day. Those few were the ones who truly cared to know and had taken the time to understand why it mattered so much to me. Ironically, I don't have much emotion associated with that actual day at Mayo. It was the first time in this process that Mayo felt emotionless. But on that day, I was simply going through the motions to get the day done with so I could get to the important part: the actual results of my recheck. I had my hearing tested, my

MRI, and a few other appointments, and then headed back home to wait for the results. They had told me that due to the time of year, I wouldn't know my results till or after the New Year, so I had roughly a two-week wait ahead.

Physically, I was still feeling fairly good a year out, but I had started to notice some symptoms sticking around a bit longer than I was comfortable with. It was small things that, right after the procedure, I would feel for a few minutes, while now they were sticking with me for closer to a full day. Every single time I would feel one of the symptoms, I would again retreat internally. I bet it was so painfully hard to read me in such moments. I'll bet all of you who loved me through this process wanted to know what I was truly feeling and thinking in those moments. I wish I could have done a better job of putting things into words, yet the words wouldn't come.

I'll bet those times that I was internal were quite obvious to all of you. Even mid-conversation with all of you, I would find myself instantly distracted by a tingling face, ringing in my ear, or a crooked feeling (if I had been walking or moving as we talked). There I was, trying to live my carpe diem values and be authentically present with all of you, yet I wasn't able to fully do so. While parts of the process felt expected and routine, I was once again, even a year later, living a life full of challenges and unexpected turns. But life continued on. Time stops for no one, and suddenly I found myself facing Christmas once again.

For some reason, I hadn't thought that Christmas might feel odd to me a year later. I was going through the motions of watching *Elf*, putting out our Christmas lights, and shopping like I always had.

In fact, I was so focused on creating an experience for everyone else, I wasn't preparing for my own personal response. I've often heard from friends how those moments come for them as well. It may be the smell of a pipe that their dad used to smoke or a certain song that comes on the radio. But our emotions are a powerful gift to our souls. When those smells and sounds take place, we are instantly teleported back to the time those memories were created.

I woke up on December 25th, and at first it felt like every other day, but I soon found that my emotions were at peak volume. Every little bit of the day made me want to cry, and I felt out of control. I was quiet as I tried to understand what was happening to me. We continued on through the morning before ending up at my parents' for our annual Christmas day brunch. The minute I sat down in that leather chair, I figured it out. The previous year, I had sat in that very chair on Christmas day and yet had no memories of it whatsoever. The only way I knew I had been there is because someone had taken a picture of me, and I remembered the image of my sunglasses and the blank look on my face. Tears began flowing down my face, and without any one else knowing, I went to my parents' bathroom and just cried. It reminded me how Herb Brooks, coach of the legendary Miracle on Ice hockey team, ran down the tunnel alone after they beat the powerful Russian team, letting his emotions flow. There are times that our emotions need to be set free, and this was one of those days.

I had come so far, and I had been through so much. I had missed an entire holiday season because of this tumor, and to this day, I remember nothing about those weeks following. Again, maybe that's best, but when I'm back in a situation that brings back those moments it feels sad. But life isn't full of just highs. Sometimes we need to embrace the lows to understand the celebration of those future highs. So I was in that bathroom, allowing all the emotions to flow, before coming back out to join the rest of the family in the living room. I didn't want to miss that moment, and I don't want to miss future moments with all of you whom I love so deeply.

The week following Christmas was slow and painful. Each day I would run to the mailbox, hoping to find a letter from Mayo with my results. Every day was a bigger letdown than the one before when the letter didn't arrive. What an odd feeling to be waiting for such important news that could take my life in so many directions outside of my control. I thought the letter would never come, and with the New Year's holiday coming, I assumed I wouldn't hear until next year. In fact, I had given up hope on the Saturday before the holiday. I was lying on the couch watching football when I heard the sound of the mailbox. I lay there wondering if it was even worth it to get the mail, and I didn't for a long time until I got up to get a drink.

On my way to the kitchen, I ran by the mailbox, grabbed the mail, and glanced down at it while walking. I came to the end of the stack and discovered it hadn't come. While I wasn't surprised, I still felt bummed. The fun part was that I received a letter from Sigma Chi, plus a few other items I was excited to read. I got my soda (pop, for you Minnesota folk) and headed back to the living room to read my mail and move on from my letdown. I picked up my Sigma Chi letter and was about to open it when I noticed that it was a bit wet from the snow that had been coming down that day, and it felt thicker than a normal letter. Right then, I noticed what had happened: the dampness had caused two letters to stick together. I pealed off the back letter, and there it was: my results from Mayo.

I paused and stared at that letter, wondering what it would say. Isn't that funny? I was holding the letter in my hand, pausing to guess what the words would tell me. It reminded me of the movie *Rudy* when he sat holding the admissions envelope that contained the results of his final attempt to get into Notre Dame. Sometimes in such moments, it feels easier to not open the envelope, but I knew it was time to face my future and my past all at once.

My emotions were building and my hands shaking as I slowly opened the letter and began to read. My mind tried to scan for the right news while also understanding the specific details of a medical letter. I finally found the words I was looking for. It had shrunk. My tumor had shrunk.

The MRI showed that blood was being cut off to that darn tumor, and it had done what the doctors had hoped. It was working, and I began to sob. All of that time and all of those appointments. All of those fearful days and missed experiences. The entire journey had come to this time-stopping moment. Time doesn't stop for anyone, but I think it did for me on that day. That cry was a release like I had never felt before, and I cried for what felt like hours. A year's worth of emotions will do that to you. The dam of emotions burst, and I simply celebrated the gift of life.

Fourteen

Speedo-Shaping Moments of Life

Our junior high years are often filled with memories that, looking back, we wish we could erase 90% of. It wasn't that junior high was bad for me, it was just awkward. Academically, I wasn't exactly a shining star, and while I had previously been good at many sports, I wasn't truly great in any one. In many ways, junior high was a search for meaning in a sea of insecurity. To add to the normal tensions of that time of life, I had stopped growing. I had always been a tall, slender kid, but during those junior high years, I was anything but.

You can imagine how going from the tall, slender kid to not growing at all impacted me, specifically my confidence. To add to the challenge, all the boys (and most of the girls) around me were physically passing me by, and I was left wondering when I, too, was going to grow. The irony during that time was that even though I wasn't growing, I was constantly hungry, so I kept eating just like my growing friends. The result of eating those many Big Macs led me to feel (and look) chubby for the first time in my life. Of course, those years would have been hard enough without that chubby feeling, but moments of insecurity just piled on top of that body and turned those years into ones I wanted to forget.

In the city I grew up in, we had six elementary schools that fed into two junior highs. So going from your safe elementary school experience to a school three times bigger was challenging enough in itself. The good part of the transition was that I had attended a camp through my church two weeks before school began. At camp, I met friends from the other schools in the city, and that helped me feel more confident walking into junior high on day one.

My counselor at camp was Ryan. He was the big brother to one of my closest friends throughout high school, Molly. He was everything a counselor should be, and his energy and joy was contagious to all of us. To create cabin bonding, he would yell "Hanny!" and hold up his hand with his index finger bent down. We saw it as a sign of unity and had no clue what it actually meant, but at that age, you don't ask; you simply enjoy the fun of the moment.

Fun was exactly what I was expecting junior high to be. All I had to compare it to was elementary school, and that had certainly been fun! So it's safe to say that I had great visions of what junior high would be like. Walking in that first day, I was instantly reminded that I had no clue how to find all of my classes. When I had gone up there a week or so before to get to know the school's layout, there hadn't been other students in the hallway! Now those giant 9th graders eclipsed the lights, and it was like being in a loud sea of confusion.

A teacher in the hall saw the fear on my face and took me aside to help. She looked at my schedule and directed me to my homeroom with Mr. Hanson. I walked in and took a seat next to a group of strangers, including Judd, who was a hockey stud in the area. He was wearing a hockey jersey from the hockey camp I had attended the previous summer, so I was thankful for something to talk about. The bell rang and interrupted our hockey bonding, and Mr. Hanson stood to speak. He waved his hand at us and introduced himself and began to explain what homeroom was and how our day would go. However, I didn't hear a word he said and I couldn't stop staring.

HOLY CRAP! I thought as I stared at the hand he had waved. *He has no index finger!*

Ryan hadn't been creating a camp bonding moment when he yelled "Hanny" with us daily: "Hanny" was Mr. Hanson! I was mortified, and the questions flew through my mind about how he could have lost it. The bell rang and we went onto our next class. I walked through the halls thinking about Mr. Hanson's missing finger.

My first class of the day was gym, and not only was I excited to be there, but I knew it was an easy class to find first. I loved courses like gym, art, and lunch in junior high because I missed elementary recess and being able to be active. But that year, with my weight gain and lack of growth, gym felt different than in previous years. I felt slow and uncoordinated, and I just couldn't do what I used to be able to. Plus, our gym teacher wouldn't tell us what lesson was next (I think it was his fun, sick control game), so we just had to show up and see what sport we were playing that day. I didn't mind the fun of the unknown until we walked into the guy's locker room to change and our teacher came out to tell us we were starting our swimming lesson that day.

We all looked around at each other and tried to process how we were going to swim with our gym clothing and no suits. He then announced, "If any of you forgot to bring your suit—" *Forgot?* I thought, *you didn't tell us!*—"you will have to use one of ours."

So we all walked over to the office where he began handing out our suits for the day: tiny green Speedos. Let me tell you, there is nothing that scars a chubby junior high boy more than walking out in front of the more mature-looking girls in a tiny green Speedo.

Let's be honest right now: junior high just wasn't going well. From scary Mr. Hanson, to a chubby body, to green Speedos, to being one of two boys in choir singing soprano, (yes…I sang soprano since I hadn't exactly gone through that "change" in my life yet) I didn't impress anyone in the junior high social world. Needless to say, the start of junior high was very different from what I had hoped for. I had had great visions for that time of my life, yet, none of them were coming true. I felt discouraged. In fact, I was far more than just discouraged: I was sad, insecure, and lost. I felt like junior high was defining me far more than I was defining it.

Life has a way of doing that. Sometimes life feels a lot like junior high. There are moments where life defines us, creating a very different world than we had expected and hoped for. While that one-page letter from Mayo had given me a new sense of hope, life wasn't aligning to that positive vision in the way I thought it would. Unlike my junior high experiences, which were bold, drastic changes, my life changes were starting to creep in almost daily, and I was struggling to react to them.

Prior to my brain tumor, whenever I met with my friends, it would always be at coffee shops. Some of you are wine snots and others are beer experts. I'm a coffee aficionado and proud of it. I love the perfect cup of coffee, and the darker the roast, the better. Even when I go to restaurants, my coffee snot lens is in place. I love to ask the server about the coffee, and if they give a generic description like, "People say it's good," I'll pass. I love the server who can tell me that it's a French Roast and even when it was roasted. So I can tell you every amazing coffee shop in the Twin Cities, the places where they truly care about their coffee. However, I found that I was starting to avoid all my favorite coffee shops, and that just wasn't like me. In the past, they gave me such joy as I sat across from a friend, drinking the perfect cup of joe.

The reality is, my body was reacting to the sounds of coffee shops, and instead of leaving those moments feeling energized, I would leave anxious and foggy. They were so loud to me. It took everything in my power to focus on the person I was with and hear what they were saying. Over time, I found myself stare at their mouth to try to understand their words over the sounds around me. But it wasn't just my ability to hear that I was struggling with: it was every sound around me that I couldn't tune out. Every drop of a spoon, grind of the coffee beans, and cough or laugh would instantly make me feel anxious. Of course I would simply try to fight through it, but when I got home and struggled to remember the conversation, I began slowly understanding that I was experiencing changes due to my procedure.

Those changes weren't just taking place in coffee shops. Sounds everywhere and anywhere would throw me off. In addition, I had as much of an emotional reaction as I did a physical reaction. Suddenly, things I had done before with great comfort and ease didn't feel the same to me. I still remember walking into church for worship and sitting down in a space I had been comfortable in my entire life. A beautiful space filled with gorgeous stained wood and large windows that let in the natural light. That space had provided years of comfort and peace for me, and I felt at home there. But the minute the music started, that anxious feeling instantly came over me. I began to fidget and then started playing with my nails. I attempted anything and everything to calm myself down, but the longer the music played, the more I began to feel confused. While I made it through the entire service, when it was done, I made a mad dash for the doors. My words felt jumbled and slurred as I tried to communicate while we drove home. That day, I went home and took a nap for almost three hours. Typically, if I nap for thirty minutes I'm proud of myself, but that day at church took every ounce of my energy.

It wasn't just coffee shops that proved challenging for me, it was any space where sound could bounce. When it did, I became confused. In fact, I began to notice that same confusion during conversations as time went on. I would experience a lag between seeing someone talk and then processing what they were saying. I also noticed the same thing when I spoke to large audiences. I've always taken great pride in my ability to interact with groups from up in front, but I started to notice changes there, too. When I asked questions from up front, I would hear a response and point to where I thought it had come from, and I would be completely off. The person who had answered would be on the exact opposite side of the room from where I had heard the sound. Of course, I would play it off and keep going, but it took a great amount of brainpower for me to refocus in those moments. Quite honestly, I felt embarrassed by it.

Over time, I also noticed that what had previously been tiny symptoms were growing into larger symptoms. It wasn't just my hearing and confusion; I also started to feel crooked. Now, I wish I could describe it better than that, but that's exactly how it felt. While you would witness me standing completely upright, it didn't feel like that to me. I felt like I was completely tilted to my left, and often when I was on my daily walks, I struggled to stay upright and not tip over. I found myself fighting my balance whenever I walked, my hips and knees would hurt more than ever before as I fought balance the entire way.

But my balance issues weren't just evident when I walked. If I turned my head too fast, I would instantly become sickly dizzy. I didn't realize what was physically happening at first, but I sure could feel the emotional reaction to such moments. One day, I was boarding a tiny plane and was walking up the stairs from the tarmac when someone to my left yelled. I quickly cranked my head to see what was happening, and next thing I knew, I was grabbing the chains on the side of the stairs and the person behind me was reaching up to catch me before I tumbled over the edge. It was a scary, insecure, and overwhelming emotional moment for me, and those same balance issues continued on the tennis court. I was completely fine hitting my forehand, but the minute I needed a quick head turn to the left to hit my backhand, I would start to tip over. Not only would I almost fall over in such moments, but if you stared at my face afterward, you could literally see my eyes still darting back and forth like I just gotten off an amusement park ride.

Though I was deeply thankful not to have facial drop or any visual problems after my procedure, there I was, years later struggling with the changes my body was still going through. What had started as slow changes early on were increasing over time. I was also struggling to sleep because of a slight ringing in my ear that would come and go early on, eventually becoming something that didn't go away. In fact, the first night I tried to sleep with that permanent ringing proved to be impossible. It was like trying to sleep with someone blowing a dog whistle in my ear all night. Over time, the volume increased, and I had to learn how to deal with a ringing that is now 24/7 for me.

Roughly a year after my last visit to the Mayo, I was back for my annual checkup, another day of hearing tests, meetings, and my annual MRI. The results of my MRI showed that my tumor hadn't shrunk any more, but it also hadn't grown. That news sure didn't feel like the previous year's letter, although it wasn't bad news either.

My hearing results, on the other hand, were where the greatest change came. I had extreme hearing loss, and I was officially diagnosed with Tinnitus. When I got my results, I immediately called Dr. Tom Christiansen, whom I consider an extended part of our family. Tom was my biking friend Eric's dad, a retired ENT, and I trust him completely. We talked for an hour, and during our call, he did a wonderful job of loving me and calming me down. One of the things he taught me is that when someone loses their hearing over time, their brain adjusts to that change since it happens so slowly.

But with how quickly I lost my hearing at such a young age, my brain had sometimes had a hard time catching up to the change. No wonder I got confused at places like conferences, church, loud coffee shops where I was struggling to understand what I was hearing!

So just like the lens I viewed junior high through, life was sure looking different than I thought it would. My physical changes were controlling me, and I was struggling to catch up emotionally to the changes. I needed to shift parts of my life that I had taken for granted for far too long. So I started making small adjustments to my life. I took up hiking and valued the chance to get outside in the quiet beauty of nature. I found the peace of a hike soothing to my soul, and it calmed my anxious spirit instantly. I also scoped out quiet restaurants and coffee shops and chose to meet friends during down times instead of busy times. Finally, I quit playing tennis, which for me was one of the most painful parts of this new world. I just couldn't do it anymore, and no matter how much balance therapy or yoga I did, I just haven't been able to stop the process of that dizzy, crooked feeling.

I was making many changes that were hard for me, and yet I was slowly adjusting to those changes. Just like that Speedo didn't define me years before, my new balance and hearing issues weren't going to define me now, either. When this process all began, I wondered if I would be defined by this tumor, and due to the gift of medicine, amazing doctors, and friends, this tumor simply provided a new perspective on life. These changes didn't define me; they are just a part of me. The good news about some of these major things I was struggling with is that there are medical solutions. So after talking to Dr. Christiansen and my Mayo doctors,

I pursued a step in the process that could help my hearing and ear-ringing in the form of a hearing aid.

I wish I could tell you that I rushed right out to set up my hearing aid appointment, but that just isn't true. To hear news at such a young age that I will need a hearing aid forever was challenging for me to process. I think my emotional reaction was due to a combination of a vain lens and a fear of the attention it would draw to me from others who don't know my story. Plus, the thought of wearing a hearing aid just made me feel old and created a new kind of insecurity. I was so impacted by this thought that, before I pursued my hearing aid appointment, I even made sure my hair was back to its longer, curly look. While I had had my hair curly and fun for years, I had made a shift to a shorter haircut for a bit of time. But once I knew I was going to get a hearing aid to help me, I quietly waited out my hair growth before I headed back down to Mayo for my appointment.

Since hearing aids aren't cheap and usually aren't covered by insurance, it can feel like a lot of money for any family to spend on one person. For me, I felt selfish at the thought of spending that kind of money on just me. I had to remind myself daily that if it would help me and my doctors were recommending it, it was a good use of money. So I set up my appointment and went through the process of trying them on and picking my color, and while I wanted to pick one with a lil bling bling, instead I went for a standard tan. The tan felt safe, and I didn't want to draw too much attention to myself (I had already done that earlier in life with my Speedo).

A week later, I picked up my hearing aid and once again was treated with nothing but perfect customer service at Mayo. I've become Mayo's biggest recruiter through this process, which has been nothing but perfect every step of the way. I was reminded weekly that the Mayo Clinic is filled with some of the most amazing, smart, life-changing experts in the world of medicine. In addition, it's filled with a team that puts the patient first, and this hearing aid experience matched every previous experience I had had with them.

You see, I wasn't just told how to use it and how to put it on, but I was also lovingly told how it would feel emotionally to wear. I walked out of the appointment and into the giant, beautiful foyer of the building and was instantly overwhelmed by all I could hear. My hearing had become so bad that I hadn't realized what I was missing, yet with my new hearing aid, I was picking up every tiny sound around me—so much so that my chest tightened in a panic. There I was, wearing my new medical gift that had cost us more money than we had, and I was so instantly overwhelmed by the feel of it, I wanted to cry.

I had never had panic attacks before, but in the early stages of wearing my hearing aid, that's exactly what was happening. Every sound felt so scary to me, and none more so than flying on an airplane. As a frequent flier, I had travel down perfectly and could teach you every trick in the book. Because of my travel expertise, I didn't think flying would be hard for me. But I was overwhelmed by how my hearing aid picked up every tiny sound: a baby crying, the air vents screaming out air, and new sounds I had never heard before. I struggled to control my breathing and tried to regain my composure. I was again having a panic attack and was so embarrassed, I didn't want to tell anyone about it. When people asked me, I tried to act like I was adjusting to it perfectly, but inside I was anything but. I hated the feel that this confident, 6'4" person was so deeply scared by every little sound. I was left to feel fear constantly, and with every new sound, my chest tightened and my breathing increased.

Weeks went on like that before I was able to get back down to Mayo. Those weeks were some of the loneliest in my life as I found myself hiding from sound as much as possible. When I was finally back down at Mayo to get my hearing aid adjusted, after sharing my emotional responses with them openly, we were able to add an on/off switch that I could quickly use if I was overwhelmed by the sounds around me. That on/off switch has proven to be a lifesaver, and in time, I also slowly began to adjust to my new hearing world. I've found that my hearing aid does indeed help mask the ringing in my ear by magnifying the sounds around me. I also began adjusting to the look of it and no longer constantly wondered if people could see it or not. But to this day, there isn't a morning that goes by that I don't think about the fact that I'm a young man wearing a hearing aid and how that feels. But I'm learning to listen to myself less. If I listen to myself, I'm often thinking negative things. Instead, I'm learning to talk to myself more because I can tell myself positives and remind myself of the good.

Of course, the good and the blessings have far outweighed the negatives. When you can't hear well, you value what you do hear even more. So I've changed, and life hasn't been exactly what I thought it was going to be, but every single day I also remind myself of the blessings of the journey. The sounds of birds and voices and laughs have never felt so beautiful. The gift of nature and the mountains have also never felt so peaceful. So while I'm a bit more crooked and still have my foggy days, I'm thankful for life. Life isn't in control of us; it gives us new paths and new journeys. Then it's up to us to choose how we will respond to it, and I choose to love life. It's that simple.

Fifteen

What's Your Story?

What's your story? Everyone has a story to tell, and as I wrote earlier, your life story is written in several books throughout your lifetime. Each book within your story matters, both to those around you daily and even to the people you have never met. We can all learn from each other and from the people who have gone before us. Sadly, we are often too busy to slow down and listen to each other's stories. Often we don't think about such things until later in life. I wish we would all learn to ask questions about each other's stories and truly listen to each other's words. Please know that your story matters, and I hope my story has had a small impact on your life.

We need to remember that your story is yours and my story is mine. By no means do I claim to know your story, and by no means do you know my full story. I gave you a glimpse of my values and one of the books of my life story, but I didn't allow you to see all of me. This was intentional; the reality is, those other parts just didn't make for a good read.

It was important for me to get this journey of my life on paper. More than anything, this book was written as a form of therapy, written as a way for my loved ones and others going through something similar to know what it felt like for me. I think more than anything, I wrote this book to share my story with the slightest bit of hope that you could not only learn from it, but also find a glimpse of hope in your own life. I've gone through something scary and life changing. It's shifted the things I can do and not do, it's shifted my values, and it's changed the lens through which I look and listen in this world. But there is more to me than this tumor, and there is more to all of you who are reading this. (Can you hear the recurring pattern?) Many of are you struggling with cancer, MS, and diseases that are far more challenging than what I have been through. Some of you may not be frozen in life as you deal with a brain tumor; rather, you are frozen as you deal with broken dreams of being a mom, husband, son/daughter, or even employee. Though I have loved sharing my story, by no means would I ever think that my tumor is any better or worse than what you are feeling. It's simply the lens I have to look through and the story I have to tell.

It's my deep hope that you will find people in your life to share your story with. By sharing our stories, we can allow ourselves to be freed from the past—both being stuck there and letting our past define us. Sadly, too many times in life people end up stuck looking backwards. It feels like you are looking at life from the taillights instead of the headlights, and trust me, I've been there. Not a day goes by where

I don't feel discouraged about parts of this process and its results. Choosing joy and choosing to live the life I want is hard but rewarding work. While I allow myself to feel such things and honor those emotions, I refuse to remain frozen.

My focus is living for today and rejoicing in tomorrow, so my story is still going strong. As my friend Dr. Shane Lopez has taught me, a hopeful lens creates forward-thinking, hopeful actions with the healthy action steps to get there. As an expert on hope, he should know all about such a lens. Shane has spent his entire life sharing hope with the world and celebrating hopeful spirits around him. In fact, it was Shane I called when I was walking out of the Mayo one day after what felt like receiving bad news. The words we use matter to those around us, especially those going through life challenges.

We all need a good reminder of hope and conversations that create a hopeful future. We need mentors who have the right words for us when we need them the most. My mentor Greg provided me with such words right after my procedure. There I was, feeling hopeless and scared, and Greg reached out in a way that was different from every other. While he allowed me to share where I was at physically and how I was feeling, he also asked me to think about the future and to tell him about the things I wanted to do. Together, in the midst of sadness, we created steps to a hopeful future. Not only that, he has come back to me over and over through the years to talk about the impact I could make and the kind of legacy I could have.

A hopeful lens begins within each of us. It's my choice every morning to choose the lens I will look at life through. My story hasn't been written for me, and I continue to be the author.

Morgan and Tyler, I started this book writing to you, and I want to end it by allowing the two of you to think about your own futures. Great mentors and friends allow us to do so, and maybe, as your dad, I can help you create futures filled with life-changing growth and world-changing impact.

In order for you to think about your own futures, I want to allow you to understand how I'm thinking about my future. Not only do I do so with a hope that there is something in my thoughts you could learn from and apply to your own lives, but also because when I'm thinking about my own future, much of it includes moments I want to share with you. I hope we can share many of my visions together. By no means will we share in all the same future values, impact, and more, but there will be some overlap.

Life is meant to be shared with others, and just as I have shared this book with you, I also want to share in life with you. You are best friends, and a life well spent will have you close to my heart and a part of those shared experiences I dream about. While I love moments like skiing in Colorado and watching a hockey game at UND with both of you, it's actually the drives there that I love more. It's in the small moments of time before and after the main event that words flow and true closeness comes.

When I think about your future and our future together, I can simply sum up my advice into two buckets: invest in yourself and invest in others. By no means am I a complex thinker, yet by thinking of those two simple statements, you can start to sort out what your future life may look and feel like. When I think about my future, those are the lenses I look through. Such statements may not tell my whole story, and they may not show all of my values, but they're simple, guiding lenses to look at life through. So starting with investing in myself, here are some things I'm thinking about in my future:

Education. As you know, I already have one master's degree in Organizational Leadership, and now am working towards a second master's in Positive Psychology Coaching (athletics.) I value lifelong learning, and I value chances to learn and grow. Education in the classroom and achieving degrees are things I value and have chosen to invest in, but I've also invested in mentors who help me learn and grow as well. Find ways to learn new things. Read books, ask questions, listen, and always think about how you can continue to grow. If you are stagnant in your life and career, it's probably because you have stopped growing. Stop blaming others and own your own learning. By taking the time to invest in your education, you will allow yourself to grow. It's that simple.

Well-being. Take care of your body and think about how you choose to eat now. The patterns you create today will be the patterns you live throughout your lifetime. The older you get, the more challenging it is to create change. I've had to learn that the hard way, but I've chosen to eat the way I do because it's best for my heart and health—and it's no surprise that it's best for you as well. Taking care of yourself will lead to a far greater possibility of enjoying a thriving future together, and if I take care to eat well now, I can have such a future as well. My new focus on eating a plant-based diet has been freeing to me. I love how I feel when I eat this way, and I love writing this book from my walking treadmill desk. By caring about what we put into our bodies, we are investing in ourselves today—an investment that will also pay off in the future.

Values. As you think about your future, let your values guide you. Take time to explore how those values continue to shift and grow. I want your values to be *your* values and not mine. Clearly, I love to talk about values, and I'm sure there are times you get tired of me doing so. But you have had the chance to be in high school while post-tumor Tom (Dad) has had values on his mind daily. So what do you value? What choices will you make because of those values? Please know that I'm asking because I want you to own and think about those values as yours. I've seen far too many people go off to college and throw out their values the minute they show up on campus. Of course, I don't think that's what truly happened, that's just how it appeared. The reality is, they never owned those values; they were living their parents' values without truly making them their own. A "values jacket" is one we put on but don't need to wear daily. True core values are those that are so deeply embedded inside of us, we can't take them off. In fact, to do so would feel foreign and inauthentic. I never want you to assume that I need you to accept my values as is. Some you may embrace and love, and some you may not. No matter what, my love for you will remain.

Exploration. Trust yourself to know what you want to see and experience, and go do it. Don't let life get in the way of embracing your drive to see and experience all that you should. There are things I know I want to experience, and I just need to do so. With that said, I've learned that I need to balance my need for adventure with a focus on stewardship (values). I've been around far too many people who were confused by how to make decisions and had a mentality of "act now and pay later." Such a mindset isn't healthy or right, and it's one that leads to greater pain than good. Our need for seeing the world can't come at such a cost that you lose sight of your values about money. Make these experiences a priority in your budget, and don't create collateral damage by your need to experience and see life.

Adventure. In terms of my own adventure, I want to go on an older wooden sailboat—called a *windjammer*—and sleep in the below-deck cabins and eat amazing meals while sitting on the deck. I want to boldly blurt out, "Where we go one, we go all!" (from one of my favorite movies). In fact, I find those words far more reassuring on a boat trip than screaming out, "I'm the king of the world!" (from a movie cruise that didn't end too well, though neither did my previously listed movie). I also want to see a football game live at Notre Dame, and I want to own a log cabin in Colorado (much of this book was written in those amazing Rocky Mountains). I tell you all of those things because, while these are things I want, you may or may not want to do them with me. But please encourage me to do them. There will be moments when I lose sight of such things, and I don't want to be old and gray, looking back and talking about what I missed out on. Invest in your dreams, go places you want to see and experience, and encourage others (including me) to do the same. You will never regret it.

Finally, let me say this: some may read my list and wonder where religion is found. As you both know, faith has guided me for my entire life, and it's the lens I look at everything through. To separate faith into its own bucket just doesn't make sense to me. In fact, I find it dysfunctional that people try to separate their faith from other areas of their life. Our faith is in all things and should be lived as such, and yet far too many live on a faith-based island. If you choose to live a life as a Christian, please don't hang out with only other Christians and listen to only Christian music. If you want to work out and do yoga, go to a place with people who have different faiths than you. If you want to learn and grow, don't go to the church as the only source of learning; go where people will challenge your thinking and make you rethink your views. We are meant to live our faith to impact others and impact our world. How can that happen if we are only hanging out with people who think the exact same way we do? My faith is a gift, and it remains at the core of who I am and what I do. But your faith will be your faith, and your lens will be your lens. When you go through something like I have, you can't imagine a world without faith.

I want you to invest in yourself, and yet sadly throughout my lifetime, I have come upon far too many people who think life is only about "investing in self." They spend their time, money, and all of their resources on ways to better themselves, yet in time, that lens becomes one of selfishness. For some, it's their faith or religion, for others it's their education, and for some it's their excessive work-out classes. All that we do in our life for ourselves should also be done so that we can impact others and the world around us. While I value and lift up investing in ourselves, I also want you to let this basic principle guide you as well: invest in others.

Investing in others starts with knowing who you are. Please don't get confused that I am calling you to only pour yourself into others. Those who pour into others for the sake of others alone without any concern for themselves can be highly dysfunctional. Take care of yourself and know yourself, and then take all that you value and share it. Allow others to experience your lens and your words, and take the time to learn the same from them. Finally, be present with others, and soak up shared experiences, embracing the gift of such moments.

Traditions. As you think about impacting others, I want you to begin by examining your own traditions and what you want to establish there. Maybe you want to walk every night as a way to get yourself moving and cleanse your mind. While that is a healthy mindset, when you think about those patterns and habits, how can they be shared with others? Instead of simply telling them that you are doing so, could you allow them to know why? Instead of keeping those healthy habits to yourself, could you allow others to take that walk with you? By so doing, you create healthy traditions that not only impact you, but impact those around you at the same time. Create traditions that are you at your best and that are centered on your core values, and then share those traditions. Invite others to your Thanksgiving dinners, buy books you value and give them as gifts to others, and use words to describe why you are doing what you are doing and why you value it so.

Time. Our values also guide who we choose to spend time with. I've sure spent a lot of time over the last few years examining friendships and how I define friends. Most of the time I have spent examining my healthy friendships is connected to how I understand the preciousness of time. Our time is limited, so who we can spend time with is precious. We are called to live life with others, but how can we sort the right people and thus the right amount of time? Let me provide you with this simple guide.

I deeply believe that we can't fully share our lives with large groups of friends. It's simply impossible to do. When we try, we spread ourselves too thin and look like a wide, shallow lake instead of a deep, rich one. Please don't get distracted by the "new and shiny" people at a cost to your true friends. While we can allow some to join us throughout our life, we need to be careful. There are two types of close friends, in my opinion. They both have a place at our table of life, and they both matter. Both types have taken the time know you, and in both cases, they were a part of one of your life books. One set of friends assumes that you are a work in progress, ever changing. The other assumes they know who you are (based on what they have seen and experienced with you in the past), and they communicate as such. It's in this small difference that I noticed the biggest change in how I have viewed friends during this season of life.

The friends I now feel closest to take the time to ask questions about how this season has changed me. They assume that since I am a work in progress, such a big episode in life would change my values and behaviors (as it clearly has). While my other set of friends, whom I still deeply care about, assume they know my values and who I am/was/will be, and have continued to treat me as that person. I find that second group to cause me more pain than the first as I try to communicate my growth and they run back to their old assumptions. True friends allow us to change, and our closest friends encourage such change. Find friends to share life with who will change with you and who will honor such changes. Find friends who will ask questions about your growth and attempt to correct the assumptions they have made about you. Those are the friends we are called to do life with and share our hearts with. Invest in them and they will invest back.

Give. As you continue to think about investing in others, I want you to consider giving your time, talents, and resources away. I want you to take care of yourself and know when you can give fully, and I do deeply hope you *want* to give. I've deeply valued giving away my money by starting a scholarship for a school and by giving back to Mayo and other brain tumor organizations. I've also valued giving my time to coach tennis and volunteer with organizations that matter to my heart. Wouldn't it be amazing to create a foundation together so that we could give to those who have given to us? I find giving so deeply rewarding and freeing that a giving vision is at the core of my values. I would love to share in forming a foundation with you and passing onto you a giving spirit so that you can impact the lives of others.

I see how much you have to give away. I look at you both and see the amazing gifts and talents you have. They are unique to you and no one else, and they make you, you. I've attempted to share my heart, life, and values with you through the words of this book and the stories of my life, and when I look at the two of you, I already see you attempting to impact freely. Already at a young age you are writing your life books and creating your own stories. What gifts those stories will be to those around you, but please be careful to not overly construct your life. If we are constantly focused on writing our future stories, we may miss the real conversations and the real life lessons that are happening around us daily.

Finally, as your dad, I simply want to say thank you to the two of you. You have both changed my life and provided the grace, love, and support to get through the moments that felt scary and overwhelming. I wish I could come up with the right words to express how deeply proud I am of you, but I can't. Instead, I will spend the rest of my life cheering for you, asking the right questions, and celebrating your lives' impact. From the bottom of my heart, please know I love you. More than words. More than life. More than any tumor. Thank you for loving your daddy back.

ACKNOWLEDGMENTS

To my Boo, who has taken every step of this journey with me:
You always knew exactly what I needed before I could find the words to ask. When I struggled to hear, you would find ways for us to go on drives and walks so we could still talk and share life. I loved how you would reach over and take my hand to calm me, and hug me perfectly when words wouldn't flow. You know me better than I know myself, and I've never felt flawed with you but always felt loved, attractive, and alive. I know you are the reason for that. Thank you for being my puzzle piece and making my life complete.

To my family who has continued to be there for me each step of the way: Thank you for ice packs, neck pillows, drives to the Mayo Clinic, allowing me to be quiet, and for honoring my moods and thoughts even when they didn't always make sense. You have all continued to be encouraging and a healthy reminder of what is important in life.

To my Sigma Chi pledge brothers, big brother, Beta Zeta brothers, former HQ staff, and Horizons and Cornerstone friends: You have continued to be a source of true friendship and have shown me time and time again what true brotherhood means. I've loved our times up the mountain and have valued your texts, calls, and e-mails. I count you as my mentors and best friends, and you help align my life to my values.

To my friends who have come from all areas of my life and from all over the country: You sent me e-mails, sat across from me at coffee shops, and constantly reminded me that I was cared for and not alone in this process. Thank you for your love and prayers.

To my Gallup friends, with whom I spend a majority of my daily life: I have loved and been honored by how you ask how I am, and have cared enough to make sure I'm taking care of my well-being. You have taught me to soar with my strengths and how to look into a mirror to understand and own my engagement and thriving life. What a gift of community you provide.

Finally, thank you to my editor Ashley Brooks who was the perfect partner. She believed in me and poured herself into making my story come alive. I couldn't have done this without her.

AUTHOR'S BIO

Tom Matson, Senior Director of Executive Leadership for Gallup's Education Practice, is an executive coach and leadership expert. Tom speaks to thousands of people each year about Gallup's research on leadership, well-being, and behavioral economics.

In 2007, Tom was appointed by former Minnesota Governor Tim Pawlenty to the Minnesota Academic Excellence Foundation, serving a two-year term. Tom has coached high school tennis for more than twenty years and was named the Minnesota Assistant Tennis Coach of the Year in 2011. He has served on the board of directors of the United States Tennis Association's Northern Tennis Foundation, the national advisory board of Tennis and Life Camps, and numerous leadership roles for the Sigma Chi Fraternity.

Tom earned his bachelor's degree in communications, master's degree in organizational leadership, and is currently completing a master's degree in positive coaching (positive sports psychology). He lives in Edina, Minnesota.

CPSIA information can be obtained at www.ICGtesting.com
Printed in the USA
LVOW06*1213120614

389775LV00004B/120/P